Do you have a book you would like to see published? Have you sent your book to agents and publishers only to have it rejected every time? Would you love to see your manuscript in a book format, but cannot afford to have it printed? If so, this book is for you.

CreateSpace.com, which is owned by the Internet book store Amazon.com, will publish your book for free. They do not require that you make any minimum purchase, and you will still own all rights to your manuscript. If you do find a publisher to publish and distribute your book, and pay you money, then you can remove your book from CreateSpace.

Until that happens, use CreateSpace to see your manuscript as a book and to give it a page on Amazon, just like Homer's Illiad. Sound too good? The catch is that you have to prepare the book to be published. You have to do all the work. You have to prepare the internal layout as well as the book cover.

This is no way as hard as it may seem. Almost any word processor can do the job to prepare the manuscript, and several types of programs, from presentation programs to drawing programs, can prepare the book cover. This book will show you how to do it using the 2007 Windows version of Word and PowerPoint. But please, to repeat, do not feel you must have those programs, there is no reasons you cannot do it with other programs. If you have some other office program, perhaps Coral Office or the free OpenOffice, this book can still be of help because it will show you what you are trying to achieve. You will have to work harder because you will have to translate the steps I take in Microsoft Office to your office program, but this book will tell you what you are trying to do.

Several other programs are also used. An inexpensive PDF creator and several freeware programs. The PDF creator is all important. There are several freeware PDF creators, which you may wish to try, but I decided to buy one because the file given to CreateSpace will be in a PDF format. The other programs used in this book, a graphic viewer and a screen clip program are freeware. In this edition of this book, I also go over how to use Coral Paint Shop Pro to create the book cover.

Using CreateSpace.com and this book, your dreams can come true.

How to Self-Publish for Free

With CreateSpace.Com

An Easy Get Started Guide

By

Jimmy Clay

CreateSpace.com

How to Self-Publish for Free with CreateSpace.Com

An Easy Get Started Guide

ISBN   1440401004

EAN-13   9781440401008

Other books by Jimmy Clay:

The Song of the Coyote

Founding Father: The Life and Times of John Neely Bryan

Check out his website at:

http://songofthecoyote.googlepages.com/

Introduction

It sounds almost too good to be true, publish for free with no minimum purchase. Nevertheless, with the exception of paying for the proof copy, which will cost around $10 depending on the size of your book, it is free. Not only that, you get your own page on Amazon. You also keep the rights to your book, so if you find a publisher willing to give you an advance for your book, you can tell CreateSpace to stop publishing the book and then sign a contract with the other publisher.

So what is the catch? The catch is that you have to do everything yourself. You have to prepare the layout of your book, choose the font, decide on the line spacing, set the margins, insert the graphics, create the cover, create the PDF files, etc. Anything that your manuscript needs to have done to it to make it look professional, you will have to do it, or it will not be done. That can be intimidating, especially if you read the instructions on CreateSpace about Adobe Acrobat or Photoshop. I know nothing about those two Adobe products, so do not worry about them. This book will use Word 2007 and PowerPoint 2007, and a few other programs to show you how to do it (but many other programs will do the job).

This book will help you get started and give you the confidence you need to prepare your book and to publish it. There is some work to it, but it will be easier than writing the book. You will need to know how to get in and out of Microsoft Word and PowerPoint (or the program of your choice), but not much else. I should add that this book is not a manual on how to use Word and PowerPoint, those are just the programs being used (they are also the programs I happen to have on my computer). This manual is illustrated and it is my goal to literally give you a picture of what you need to do.

Introduction

If you do not own Word 2007 or PowerPoint 2007, do not feel you have to rush out to buy them. You should be able to achieve the same goals listed in this book using other programs. It will be easier if you do have Word 2007 and PowerPoint 2007 because you will be able to follow the steps, but Word 2003 and PowerPoint 2003 should be able to do it. Coral Office and the free OpenOffice are two other programs that might work. This book is an example of how you can go about getting your book published; it is not an attempt to tell you the only way it can be done.

In addition, this book has nothing to say about how you write the book. This book is not about writing; this book is about getting published for free. If you have a manuscript, then you are good to go. If you are still working on your manuscript, this book will give you hope that you will be able to see the book in a book format and on Amazon.

This book has three parts. In the first part, the overview, I want to give you some idea of where you are going and give you some confidence that what you are going to do is not that hard. The second part is a step-by-step example on how to prepare the internal material for publishing. The internal materials are the words and pictures in your book, and I will give you ideas how to make them look professional. This section will show how one book was published, that book being my coyote novel, *The Song of the Coyote*. You do not need to buy my novel to benefit from these instructions, although I would love it if you did (I thank highly of my novel). I will provide screen shots of the steps I took to prepare my novel, and you can use Amazon's preview feature see how my book turned out. The third part will show you how to prepare your book cover. Turns out, that is not hard to do. In fact, it might be the most fun part of the process. Although developing the design is hard.

In addition to using my coyote novel as an example, I will point out some of the things about this book, the one you are now reading, that might be of interest, but preparing this book was the same as for my novel. This book is much the same except that it uses different parameters—different book size, different margins, different fonts, etc. Also in this book, I used many screen clips and lists, and I will explain how I prepared them.

I hope you find this book helpful. Remember, there is no need to do everything exactly as I did them. I am helping you get started by giving you the benefit of my experience and telling you how I created my books. You can be different; you can choose whatever book size you want from the choices provided by CreateSpace, you can decide how big you want your margins, what kind of headers you want, and so on.

One warning: I am using my coyote novel as an example, but I cannot guarantee that I will not change that novel, so the examples may not correspond exactly to the novel. For example, the pricing of my novel could change and I may redo the cover using Coral Paint Shop Pro. The examples are only to help you understand and they should stay valid for that purpose.

Another warning: CreateSpace is constantly changing their website to improve it. Do not be surprised if the website is not reflected in this book perfectly. It can change without warning.

Overview

What is CreateSpace?

CreateSpace is the great hope for all want-a-be writers, such as me and perhaps you. For almost no cost, you can have your book—fiction or nonfiction—setup for on-demand publishing. It will have its own page on Amazon, and Amazon will sell it like any other book. If a customer comes across your book while browsing Amazon, and if they like what they see, they can order it from Amazon. Amazon will send the order to CreateSpace, who will then print it, bind it, and send the book to the customer.

Notice that Amazon and CreateSpace do not go to a warehouse to retrieve a copy of your book. This is because your book will not exist in a paper form until a customer places an order. Until then, it is merely stored as a PDF file in one of CreateSpace's computers. Only when the customer places an order is your PDF file sent to the printer, where your book will be printed and bound for that one order. Amazon completes this process for each order. Please be aware that your book will not be distributed to bookstores.

Seems like a lot of trouble. However, with the cost of computers and disk storage falling to almost nothing, and as printing technology increases—lowering printing cost and increasing printing reliability—this might be the future of all books. It does not take too much imagination to foresee a day when all books will be printed on-demand and the only books being stored in a paper format will be the books in bookstores. The exception being books selling in exceptional quantities, such as the Harry Potter novels.

CreateSpace is an on-demand publisher. They publish DVD's, CD's, Audio books, and other on-demand products, which you can review by visiting their website at www.createspace.com. For our purpose, what is important is that they will make your book available for printing. Also, and this is very important, they are owned by Amazon. This gives CreateSpace a measure of stability that other on-demand publishers do not have. It makes one feel confident that they will not go out of business anytime soon, and it cannot be overstated that you will get a web page on Amazon.com, one of the biggest booksellers in the world.

As I already mentioned, the major catch is that you have to do all the work. This differs from traditional printing because if a major publisher publishes your book or if you pay an on-demand publisher to print your book, they will do the layout of the internal material, and they will design the cover (all you have to do is write the book). CreateSpace will not do any of that for you. You have to do all those things yourself. You have to prepare the layout of your book and create the file that CreateSpace will use to print your book. You have to design the book cover and create the file that CreateSpace will use to print the cover. All CreateSpace will do is store your book's files, give it a page on Amazon, see that it is printed when an order is placed, then keep up with yours and theirs earnings.

How do they make money on your book? You might think the answer is obvious, from the sale of your book to thousands of customers. The reality is that very few people, unless you can find some way to market your book, will buy your book. That is the harsh reality. If that is the reality, that you cannot expect to sell many books, how does CreateSpace make money? First, I had to order numerous proofs before I got my book right, each costing around $9.19, spending in all around $60. Second, when I finally finished, the first thing I did was order 10

copies. The price was $9.19 per book, $10 for shipping, so I spent $101.90. With the cost of storage on disk being almost nothing, and printing being so efficient, I am sure they are making a profit. I should add that I earned no earnings from the proofs or the books that I bought for myself.

You might wonder what makes up that price of $9.19. As I will show you later, the retail price is derived from several parts. The $9.19 I paid was made of just two of those parts—first the fixed charge and second the per page cost. (For my coyote novel when it was published, the fix charge was $3.15, and the charge per page was 302 pages x $0.02 = $6.04. The $3.15 plus the $6.04 equals $9.19.) Notice that you are not paying CreateSpace the 20% they would have made if you had bought from their E-Store, nor or you paying the 40% you would have paid if you had bought from Amazon. This is a great deal. The charges will change (probably upward), so check with the CreateSpace website to get the current details.

If preparing your book sounds hard, it can be, but only if you do not know what you are doing. Helping you get started is what this book is all about. I will explain all the steps I took to publish my novel, *The Song of the Coyote*. I will keep no secrets from you. I will also provide information on this book, the one you are reading, that you may find interesting. I will go over the page layout, cover design, and creating the PDF files. We will do it without buying any costly commercial publishing programs, which can cost $600 or more.

Is it really free?

Good question. My answer is yes, but it depends on how you define free. All I had to pay CreateSpace was the cost of the proofs. The proof is the first copy of your book to be printed. After you upload your files to CreateSpace, they will review it (this is called preflighting) for problems. If there are none, then you have to order a proof, review it—and if you decide it looks fine—you then tell CreateSpace to make it available for sell; you do this by logging into your account and clicking the okay button. They then send the information about your book to Amazon and it will go on sell. If you do not like the way the proof looks—for whatever reason—then you can make the necessary changes to your manuscript, create another PDF file, and upload it again. You will then have to order (and pay for) another proof of your book. You keep doing this until your book meets with your approval. As I said, I did this numerous times for my coyote novel.

For the first proof of my novel, I paid them $9.27, plus $5.50 for shipping, making it $14.77. I had to do this again because I saw little things that I thought I could improve on. So I made my changes, uploaded it again, and order a second proof copy for $9.19 (they had a special going on and I did not have to pay for shipping, also the unit cost was $0.08 less because somehow I reduced the page count by four pages). Then when I saw the second proof, I discovered more stuff that needed to be changed; a small list of little problems. The third proof also cost $9.19 because I did not have to pay shipping. However, I now discovered that some of the clip art I was using was not royalty free; the clip art had not been licensed for use in any product being sold. So I took the offending art out, replaced them with non-offending art, and ordered a fourth proof. The fourth proof looked great, except the cover graphic was off centered, so I ordered a fifth proof. Luckily, I did not have to pay shipping for the last four proofs.

Compare that to the $15 I paid to have my Coyote novel printed at an office supply store; and that $15 was pretty cheap; other places—such as a well-known company that will print and ship it—wanted around

$30 (just for the printing), and these companies are just using standard printer paper, with no binding or cover. For $9.27, I am getting a bounded copy of my book with graphics and a nice cover.

Is it free? I am after all paying at least $9.19 per proof, and I had to do it many times. I will just say that CreateSpace publishes for free; they do not print for free. They must be making some kind of profit on this, but I do not know how much. I had another book published with a different on-demand company and that book, *Founding Father: The Life and Times of John Neely Bryan*, cost almost $1000 to publish (I did get ten paperback and one hardback book for that $1000). Does CreateSpace deliver free demand service? Yes. But if you want to see it in print, you will have to pay.

A future for free publishing?

Is this the future of publishing? I hope so because for once I want to be leading the way instead of following. It makes sense that it would be the future because storing books in a warehouse cost money and many books sit in inventory for years until they are finally sold out. With on-demand printing, the book sits in a computer until someone orders it, then it is printed.

If free print on-demand does become the future for writers, this presents an interesting problem. If anyone can be printed, even someone who has written trash, how can we sort out the small amount of good stuff from the large amount of not so good stuff? The big publishing houses probably will still be around just as they are now. They will select the books they like and market them just as now and pay the lucky author for the right to do so. The difference is that they will not publish thousands of copies of a book at once; they will publish only enough to meet a current order.

One change might be that those publishing houses will be able to market more books, because they will not have to invest in large printings. Without the risk and cost of having to print and warehouse so many copies of each book on their list, they should be free to increase the diversity of the books they sell. However, they will still market a limited number of books, a number that they can market efficiently.

The rest of us who are not picked will still be left on our own. The good news is that we can get published and we can do it for free. If nothing else, this is fun and a wonderful ego trip. But we would like to be read, and many of the books published in this way will deserve to be read. Yet the number of books published will be astronomical. Remember, anyone can do it. Some of those books will be great, but those great ones will be few among thousands of other books being self-published and offered by companies like Amazon on the Internet. How do we find and pick out the great ones from all the others?

I do not know.

I suspect that at least two things will have to happen. The companies that offer on-demand services will have to take an active role in searching for the great books. They see these books and will have to take note when a great one is in their mist. This will be to their own advantage because they will also make money from these books if more of them are sold.

The second solution is the book reading community. This is a little harder because most of us cannot order self-published books at full price just to see if they are any good. Instead, we need a hint they are worth buying. Amazon already allows for the preview of the first few pages of all books that CreateSpace publishes. (Amazon's preview

displays the front cover, table of contents, copyright page, the first several pages of chapter one, the back cover, and the surprise me feature). A good start, but eventually, especially for books that cannot be bought in bookstores, more previewing is necessary. One possibility is to allow potential readers to scroll through the whole book, perhaps there should be a fifteen- or thirty-minute time limit. Then, if the customer does order the book, and they like it, we can hope they will return to Amazon and submit a comment to let the world know. Still if one book, among thousands, gets a good review, I am not sure why anyone would notice it, unless there is a central page listing the best reviews.

Amazon is doing a good job providing ways for readers to discuss books. But like independent films, independent books will have to develop a loyal readership. Maybe eventually, Amazon will create a page just for independent books where lists can be made of the top independent selling books and where readers can rate them. Perhaps other websites and communities will develop where great self-published books are reviewed and discussed.

Print on-demand, especial free print on-demand, presents an opportunity for want-a-be writers to see their efforts in print. Just as important, it presents the possibility that truly great works of art that otherwise would not be published will be. How those great books will be sorted out and found I am not sure, but I am sure that free publishing is something most of us will like.

Who is the author?

I do not work for CreateSpace or Amazon; in fact, as I write these words they do not know I am working on this book. I plan to surprise them. Like you, I am an author looking to be published. I have not been published by any large publishing house. My experience is that I did pay once to have a novel published, and I published my novel *The Song of the Coyote* with CreateSpace, and there is this book. Including this book, I have written four books. The fourth, which I have not mentioned is called *Jerime*; it has not been published anywhere, but I hope to eventually publish it with CreateSpace.

I admit that I do not have the best credentials for writing this book. I have not worked in the publishing industry, and I know little about the Adobe products and Quirk Express, expensive desktop publishing programs. But I do have two things going for me. I did get a novel successfully published with CreateSpace—I am talking about *The Song of the Coyote*—and I got this book published also with them. That shows I do know how to do it. What I am going to do in this book is show you what I did.

I am simply going to tell you how I did it. There are other ways to do it, maybe better ways. My hope is to get you going, point you in the right direction, and to help you get past the intimidation you might be feeling, and show you that preparing the files for uploading to CreateSpace is not so difficult. I will encourage you to experiment and create a look for your book. The best thing about CreateSpace, besides the low cost, is that you are in control of your book.

What are your options?

You have many options when publishing your book. The first two options are the design of the inside of the book and the design of the cover. You have to decide how you want them to look, so start thinking. Just to help you get started, I suggest you find a book— in your own book collection, the library, or a bookstore— that has a look that you

want to emulate. Once you find this book, there will be no need to emulate it exactly, but it will help you get started.

For my novel, I chose to emulate the look of my first book, *Founding Father: The Life and Times of John Neely Bryan*. This was a start, but as I studied the font in that book, I decided that it was too intense and small and dense for the teenagers who would be reading my coyote novel. Then one day I was looking in the book section of a large discount superstore, and found an appropriate book that had larger fonts and line spacing. I was now emulating my first book on some things and this second book in others. You may have to experiment to emulate another book because you will not know how the affects of that book were created. I experimented with the fonts and the line spacing in my coyote novel and in the process came up with my own font combination and line spacing that I liked.

For this manual, I found an old computer book on Microsoft Word 2002. I liked it because it used large fonts and lots of white space, which made the material in that manual seem less intimidating. It also used screen clips to illustrate the steps. I tried to do both of those things in this book. Emulating is a tool to get started, but do not be bound by it, let your book evolve.

What your book will look like is the first thing you need to consider. The next consideration is if to publish in black and white or in color. Unless you are publishing a very small book, I suggest you publish in black and white. A book published in color will cost much more. A book in color will cost three times more than a black and white book.

The next choice will be the size of the book. Since I published the first edition of this book, CreateSpace has double the choices of book size. You have to choose a size that they have listed. Take a look at their website to see what they currently offer. Let the type of book you are publishing determine its size. If you have a small volume of poetry, you will want to use a smaller size; if you are doing a textbook with high word count and many diagrams, you might need a bigger size.

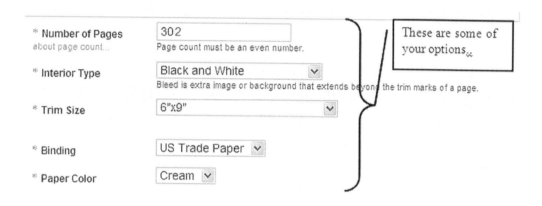

The next choice will be between cream or white paper. Do you want the paper in your book to be plain white or do you want it to be a little off white. It is like deciding if to paint the walls of your house white or antique white. I was going through the books I own, looking at the page colors, something I never paid attention to before, and I found books that were white and books that were cream. One trend I noticed is that novels tend to be cream and nonfiction tends to be white. I do not know if that is a rule or not, but it seems to be. I cannot say that either color is better than the other, but I went with the cream for my coyote novel because it is a novel. This book that you are reading now is printed on white paper. One thing of interest is that cream paper is thicker than white paper and that will be important when we create the book spine for the cover.

Last, pricing is fun to consider. When I talk about the price, I am referring to how much you charge for each copy of the book. When I talk about the charges for your book, I am talking about how much of that price CreateSpace keeps.

Over the half year that I first published this book and my coyote novel, the way CreateSpace charges has changed. Please check their website for up to date details. As I write these words, July 2008, the pricing is based on the number of pages your book has, if it is non-color or color, and if you subscribe to the Pro Plan or not. It also depends on whether the E-Store or Amazon sells your book. For this example, we will consider a book sold by Amazon. The first table will assume that you did not subscribe to the Pro Plan and the second will assume you did. Notice how much more you have to charge for the color book, to make the same profit as for the B&W book. For my coyote novel:

Black and white option	Color option
Pages > 302	Pages > 302
Book cover price > $13.95	Book cover price > $64.70
Amazon's percent 40% > $5.58	Amazon's percent 40% > $25.88
Fixed cost > $1.50	Fixed cost > $1.75
Cost for pages $0.02 x 302 > $6.04	Cost for pages $0.12 x 302 > $36.24
CreateSpace's cut > $13.12	CreateSpace's cut > $63.87
My profit > $0.83	My profit > $0.83

What about the Pro Plan? The Pro Plan will let you make a higher profit on each book sold. The question you have to ask is if you will sell or buy enough books to recover the cost of subscribing to the Pro Plan, because you do have to pay extra for it. Currently the cost of the Pro Plan is $39, but I am sure that will go up, so check the website for the new price.

Here is the same table as above, but using the Pro Plan:

Black and white option	Color option
Pages > 302	Pages > 302
Book cover price > $13.95	Book cover price > $43.15
Amazon's percent 40% > $5.58	Amazon's percent 40% > $17.26
Fixed cost > $0.85	Fixed cost > $.85
Cost for pages $0.012 x 302 > $3.62	Cost for pages $0.07 x 118 > $21.14
CreateSpace's cut > $10.05	CreateSpace's cut > $39.25
My profit > $3.90	My profit > $3.90

To benefit from the Pro Plan, for a B&W book, it would have to sell 24 copies to break even. CreateSpace has a pricing spreadsheet on their website that will let you play with different prices and see how much money you will make.

Some requirements

There are some requirements we have to keep in mind. First, please remember that every graphic inside the book or on the cover, has to have a 300 DPI (that is dots per inch). Believe me, we will go over this. Let me warn you about one thing that you need to do in both Word and PowerPoint. That is to set the compression options to <u>not</u> compress the graphics during save (I will show you how). Never, never, never compress your pictures or graphics because that will lower the DPI. I made this mistake with the first file I uploaded. The clip art when I

inserted them into my manuscript was set at 300 DPI, but when I saved the manuscript, Word automatically compressed the art to a lower setting. I had to reinsert all my graphics into the manuscript, re-create the PDF file, and upload them again.

CreateSpace has certain book sizes that they will work with. You must pick one of those sizes, not something in between. You must set the page layout of your Word manuscript and your PDF Creator to the size you choose.

The next thing is that the page size of the PowerPoint slide with the book cover has to be set to a width of eighteen inches and a height of twelve inches (18 x 12, always in inches). No matter what book sizes you choose, this will be true. If the book size is small, this slide will have a lot of white space going around it. If the book size is bigger, there will be less white space. If you decide to create your book cover with some other program, such as Corel Paint Shop Pro, the final file you create will have to be 18 x 12.

The next thing to remember is that the book cover must be position **exactly** in the centered of the slide. There should be a well-proportioned white border going all around it. This is as important as anything said in this book. If you do not center it correctly, when they cut the cover out of the 18 x 12 piece of paper, it will not cut correctly. Some of the cover will go with the trash paper and some of the white paper will become part of the book cover. Related to that here is a caution about PowerPoint. PowerPoint will not lock your design to the center. You have to be careful that you do not accidentally move it.

About the spine, there is a formula for calculating the spine's width, and there will be a small difference depending on whether you choose to print the book with white or cream paper. Once you have completed the book's layout, you will know the number of pages the book will have and can then calculate the spine's width. There is some simple math involved here, but not much. I will show you how. As part of the setup, CreateSpace will ask you how many pages your book has; they will then calculate the spine's width for you. Use their calculation to check your calculation.

We will go over all these things again. Right now, I am just trying to frame your thinking. You have a lot of latitude as to what you do with your book, even if they are the wrong things to do. These are a few of the things that you must pay attention to.

Let me go over the above point, "even if they are the wrong things to do." CreateSpace will do some basic checks—the preflight of your PDF files—to help you get your book right. This preflight check is concern only with the PDF file and with making sure that it will print on a commercial printer. For everything else—usage, grammar, spelling—it is all up to you to do it right. If you insert a graphic in your book or cover and it turns out all black, do not expect them to take care of it. It is up to you to do so. Everything is up to you. Do not call CreateSpace for help. But on their website they do have a community where you can ask questions and people like you will give their best answer based on their own experiences. Give them a try.

Programs that I used

I recommend that you buy a soft tape measure, such as the ones used on clothes. It needs to be soft so you do not risk scratching your monitor. You will use this to measure the size of your book on the screen. If you decide to create a book that is six inches wide, when you view it at 100%, it should be six inches on your monitor. Word has a ruler that you can use, but I would not trust it; I would measure it with

your tape measure. Be sure. You might also find the tape measure useful for measuring all sorts of things, such as graphics and white spaces.

The two main programs use in the examples in this book are the 2007 editions of Microsoft Word and PowerPoint. There is no reason you cannot do everything that is needed using the Microsoft Office 2003 editions, other office programs, or inexpensive paint programs; but this book is illustrated with Office 2007. Office 2007 uses ribbons and not the menu system 2003 uses, but the dialogue boxes are close to being the same as Office 2003. If you decide to use some other program, skim this book to learn what you are trying to do, then go find out how to do the same thing in your program.

With the 2003 edition, you will need a PDF creator (which is a type of software); you will also need one with the 2007 editions. The Office 2007 program does have a PDF add-on that you can download from the Microsoft Office website. This PDF add-on has few options that can be set, and it compresses the PDF files and changes the DPI of the graphics. I do not have confidence in it. I tried a few freeware PDF creators by did not have confidence in them either. I finally decided to buy one. There are a number of them that you can buy, but the one I bought is novaPDF. It comes in several versions. I bought the standard version because I wanted to be able to save profiles. To create the PDF files to upload to CreateSpace, you need a good PDF creator because the PDF file is all-important, so get a good one.

Three other programs that I used are the freeware programs, IrfanView, PrintKey 2000 and MWSnap. I used IrfanView on both books. IrfanView is a graphic viewer that can set the DPI level, can resize graphics, can resample the graphics (which we will talk about later), and save the graphic to a TIFF format. PrintKey 2000 and

MWSnap are programs I used to make all the screen clips that are in this book. PrintKey 2000 is the program I used to make the screen clips of the first edition of this book, but that program was discontinued, so I have switched to MWSnap for this book. You can download IrfanView and MWSnap over the Internet. To find their home website, do an Internet search with Google or Yahoo. In the steps I outline below, I am going to assume you have these programs installed on your computer. If you are using other programs, you will have to translate the steps I give to your program. Of course, if you are not using screen clips in your book, you will not need MWSnap, but you will need a program like IrfanView to create your cover.

Finally, the clip art programs. Before you buy any clip art, make sure it is royalty free because they each have their own licensing agreement. I have learned the hard way that not all clip art is licensed for on-demand books. Some popular collections stipulate in their licensing agreement that their clip art cannot be used in anything that is to be sold. I used a lot of clip art with my coyote novel. I love clip art and bought three collections, in addition to the Microsoft Office collection. Turns out, I could not use one of them. Worse, the graphic I loved the most, which I used on the cover, was making me into a criminal. Worse still, I did not discover this until I published the book and bought ten copies.

CreateSpace does allow you to place your title on hold, which will stop the sell and production. Then you can redo your book and upload it, which is what I did with my novel (and what I am doing to create the second edition of this book). Of course, you will have to pay for another proof copy.

The royalty free clip art I bought was Hernera's The Big Box of Art 410,000 and two Dover Clip Art CD's. With The Big Box of Art 410,000,

you can copy the clip art from the CD's to your hard drive. This package has a browser that will help you to convert the clip art to the size, DPI, and format that you need. The Dover Clip Art is very high quality and they let you use ten of their clip arts per book. I also used several clips from the Microsoft collection and one public domain clip. Remember, if you use these programs or any other royalty free program, to give them credit on your copyright page (something else I did not do the first time).

I want to emphasize that you do not have to use the same programs that I am using. What I am doing with Word, PowerPoint, NovaPDF, and the other programs, I am sure many other programs can accomplish. If you choose to use different programs than what I am using in this book, you will have to read your program's instructions to find the steps I relate in the book, and you will learn more about your program in the process.

What are the steps to getting published?

I am going to try to give you an idea about the steps that you will have to take with CreateSpace. But before we get started, the first thing you need to know is that you will not be asked for a credit card number until you are ready to order the proof copy of your book (unless you select the Pro Plan option). Knowing that, you should feel at ease. To get started, you will need to create an account. Go to their website at www.createspace.com. Click the **Sign up now** button. You will have to give them your name and email address and create a password. Your email address will be your username.

I signed up with them over a year ago, and as I write this, I have yet to receive any strange emails or spam. I feel you can give them your email address without any worry. Next, click the **Create your account** button. When you do that, you will be taken to the service agreement. I am not a lawyer, so I can give you no advice here. You will either have to agree to it or go no further.

If you agree to the terms and conditions of the service agreement, you will be given a member ID number and will be taken to the **Member Dashboard**. For now that is all you have to do; although I expect you will want to click some of the links and explore the CreateSpace website.

One link you will want to click on is under the **My Products** section. Click where it says **Click here to create a title**. This will take you to a page where you can select what kind of product you want to create. Click where it says **Paperback Book**. This will take you to the first phase of the upload process. You do not have to fill this page in now, but it is nice to see it. Look at it to get some ideas about what you will have to do later.

You need to start thinking about what you are going to write in the fields on this page. Such as how you are going to describe your book, how you are going to describe yourself, the five search words you want to give your book, and the book's category. The ISBN and EAN numbers will be assigned to your book when you save the Title Information. (The ISBN and EAN numbers are for your book like the bar code number is for merchandise at your local department store.) You will have these numbers and can copy and paste them to the copyright page (this will make your book look more professional).

One more important note: Please notice that some of the items on this first page you cannot change after you publish the book. One such item is the title of your book. So do not misspell it.

If your book already has an ISBN and an imprint, you can enter them here. If you need help with this, you will have to email the CreateSpace help team because I did not have to deal with this. If you do not have an ISBN or an Imprint, let CreateSpace assign you one, which is what I did.

Now we will go through the rest of the steps so you will know what you can look forward to. Assume that you have finished preparing your book. After you have filled in all the information on this first page, click the **Save and Continue** button and you will be taken to the next step.

* Title	The Song of the Coyote
	This cannot be changed after you submit this book for publishing.
Subtitle	
	This cannot be changed after you submit this book for publishing.
Volume Number	
	This cannot be changed after you submit this book for publishing.
* Description about the description...	Join Tyke and her brother Dingo—two young coyotes—as they play, learn, explore, and set out on adventures. Watch as Tyke learns the ways of the Great Coyote and as Dingo falls in love. Experience the emotions of success and tragedy. And learn the meaning of heroism. You may enter a maximum of 1,000 characters in book description field.
* ISBN what's this?	⦿ Assign my book an ISBN-13/EAN-13 immediately. IMPORTANT: If you select this option, an ISBN-13/EAN-13 will be immediately assigned to your book upon clicking the Save & Continue button at the bottom of this page. Once the page has been saved, the selection cannot be changed. ○ I already own an ISBN-10 for this book. 1434812081 This cannot be changed after you submit this book for publishing. ○ I already own an ISBN-13/EAN-13 for this book. 9781434812087 This cannot be changed after you submit this book for publishing.

Here you will be asked how many pages your book has, if it is going to be a black and white or if it will be color, what size the book will be, the binding (as I write this, the binding has to be US Trade Paper, but check the website for new options), and if you want white or cream paper. Please note that you will not know the number of pages until you have finished the page layout, which is what much of this book is about. You can change this information until you click the final button to publish, then you cannot make any changes. When you are finished with this page, click the **Save and Continue** button.

Next, you finally get to upload your files. You will have two PDF files, one for the cover and one for the internal materials. Click the upload button for your internal files, browse to and select your internal PDF file, click the **Open Button**, and then click the **Upload Button**. (Be sure to upload the correct file). Next do the same thing to your cover PDF file. The maximum size for your internal PDF file is currently one hundred megabytes. The maximum size of the cover PDF file is currently forty megabytes.

Uploading can take a long time, so be patient. I believe it took my files almost forty-five minutes. I suggest that you not use your computer while this processes. If your computer is working on something else, such as downloading files, wait for that to stop before you upload your book. Once you upload both PDF files, click the **Save and Continue** button.

Once that step is finished, you will be asked to give a price to your book. There is a minimum price that you can charge, which is calculated for you and you will see it. If you charge this minimum price, you will make no profit. You might think that anything above this

minimum will be your profit, but that is not correct. Amazon, when they sell your book, gets a percentage of the price you charge, so the more you charge the more they get too. Do not worry about that, simply put down a reasonable price. You may want to look at the prices of other books that are similar to yours. You can change this price later, even after you have submitted your book for sell.

You will be given the opportunity to subscribe to the Pro Plan. If you click this option, you will be taken to the check out page to pay for it. But, and this is important, you do not have to buy the Pro Plan at this time. You can wait to do so later.

Below where it says "Amazon.com Retail Sales" there is a down arrow for "Browse Keywords." Click that box and choose the selection that is best for your book.

This page will also show you how much money you will get for each book sold. How much you make will depend on if the book is sold by Amazon or by the CreateSpace's E-Store. You will notice that it will pay

to get people to buy from the E-Store. This above example is from my coyote novel.

Click **Save Changes** and you have finished for now. You will be taken to a page where you can review your answers. Change them if you need to. When you have finished, click the **Save and Continue** button.

Now you will go to a page that says **Summit for Publishing**. Take a deep breath and click the button that says **Summit for Publishing**. Once you do that, you have finished for a day or so.

You now have to wait for the files that you uploaded to go through a preflight test. Preflight is the examining of your PDF files to make sure they fulfill the minimum requirements. CreateSpace has a preflight program that will examine your PDF files. Remember, they are checking for the basic requirements. They are not checking to see if your book should be published. You will be emailed, probably the next day, and told if there were problems or if your files are okay. The first file I uploaded had problems with the graphics not set at the proper DPI of three hundred and it had transparencies. I fixed those problems and my next file I uploaded was corrupted. On the third try, no problem was found. I found this preflight step to be the most difficult. It can be frustrating, if they are having problems with your file, to discover what the problem is. CreateSpace will not solve this problem for you; this is one of those things you have to do yourself. My best advice here is to make sure that your word processor file, the one you use to create you PDF file from, contains no macros or add-ins, just words, format, and graphics. And use a good PDF creator program.

At the end of this section, you can read the first email they sent me to tell me I had a problem, then the email they sent when I finally solved the problems. When they send you an email saying there are no

problems, you can then order your proof. This is when you will be asked for money (unless you chose the Pro Plan option).

Now you have to wait and wait for your proof to be delivered. The proof, just to be clear, is the first printed copy of your book and will be how your book will look to anyone who orders it. You need to make sure it is what you want because you will have to live with it. When a customer orders your book from Amazon, the book they get will look like the proof you have (if you approve it). If you do not like the proof, you do not have to approve it.

If you do not like it, you will have to make the necessary changes to your Word manuscript or PowerPoint file, create another PDF file, and upload it again, wait for the email saying the PDF files are okay, and then reorder (and pay for) another proof. You will have to keep doing this until you are happy. If it is the cover you are unhappy with, you will have to upload only that one file, same if it is the internal material. However, if you have concerns with just one of them, you still have to buy the whole proof.

When you are happy, you will then approve the proof and then a web page will be created for your book on the Amazon website, and it will be made available for preview and sell. Your book will have a web page on Amazon just as Harry Potter does. The Amazon page will be created quickly, but the whole process of putting a picture of your book and the preview files on the web page might take six to eight weeks. Be patient.

Once your book is on Amazon with a web page, you will still be free to put your book on hold, stopping the sell and production of it. You might do this if you sign a contract with a publisher who will distribute your book. Or you might create a better book cover. Or you may decide to update your book, such as I am doing here. Or for any other reason you might have.

And that is all there is to that.

However, before you do the above, except for creating your CreateSpace account, you will need to prepare the book's page layout. You need to make your book look professional. Then you need to design your book cover.

The first files I submitted to CreateSpace had problems. Here is the email they sent me:

The interior and cover files for The Song of the Coyote have been reviewed and are printable in their current state.

The interior file contains transparency. Transparency will be manually flattened during our processing and may cause a color shift.

The cover file contains transparency. Transparency will be manually flattened during our processing and may cause a color shift.

The interior file contains images at 199 DPI, which will appear blurry and pixilated in print. For optimal printing, we recommend all images be at least 300 DPI

The cover file contains images that range from 198 to 220 DPI, which will appear blurry and pixelated in print. For optimal printing, we recommend all images be at least 300 DPI.

You may upload new files or you may proceed with the publishing process using the current files.

If you would like to upload new files, you may wish to review the Submission Requirements, available under the Books section on the Help tab.

If you wish to proceed with the publishing process using the current files, your next step is to order your book's proof copy. To do so, log in to your CreateSpace member account, click on the shopping cart icon corresponding to your book and follow the on-screen instructions. Please note you will need to click "Confirm Order" for us to receive your order. Your proof copy will be printed and shipped to its final destination.

If you are completely satisfied with your proof copy when you receive it and are ready to make your book available for sale, log in to customflix.com member account and click the edit (pencil) icon corresponding to your book. Review your book's information for accuracy and click "Approve Proof" to make your book available for sale. Your book will soon appear for sale through the selected distribution channels.

If you are not completely satisfied with your proof copy when you receive it, you may make any necessary changes to your files, upload them again and order another proof after those files have been reviewed.

When I fixed all the problems, and I uploaded again, they sent an email that looked like this:

Congratulations, the files for The Song of the Coyote have been reviewed and meet the submission specifications. The next step in the publishing process is to order your book's proof copy. To do so, log in to your CreateSpace member account, click on the shopping cart icon corresponding to your book and follow the on-screen instructions. Please note you will need to click "Confirm Order" for us to receive your order. Your proof copy will be printed and shipped to its final destination.

If you are completely satisfied with your proof copy when you receive it and are ready to make your book available for sale, log in to your CreateSpace member account, and click the edit (pencil) icon corresponding to your book. Review your book's information for accuracy and click "Approve

Proof" to make your book available for sale. Your book will soon appear for sale through the selected distribution channels.

If you are not completely satisfied with your proof copy when you receive it, you may make any necessary changes to your files, upload them again and order another proof after those files have been reviewed.

Preparing the Internal Material

Layout considerations

Here is a suggestion: If your manuscript has macros and add-ins, I suggest that before you start preparing the final layout of your book that you copy it from the original file into a new file. The idea here is to put your book into a file that has never seen a macro or add-in. I am superstitious about the preflight of the PDF files and have had some problems getting my PDF files passed the preflight. This step will remove one potential problem.

The first thing I recommend you do is to find another book to emulate, perhaps one that is the same type or genre as yours. I am not suggesting that you should copy every detail of it; instead, what I am suggesting is that you use that book as a way to get started. As your understanding grows, no doubt you will see things you will want to do differently, and you might also find that circumstances will force you to do things differently.

One of those circumstances is the number of words you have to work with. If your story is a long one, you may need to use a smaller font and have smaller margins to keep the number of pages down. After all, each page drives up the price of your book. On the other hand, if your story is short, with few words, you might need to make your fonts bigger and your margins larger to fill up space (so your book will look like a book).

If you are writing for people who are in their retirement ages, you might want to use larger fonts with larger spaces between the lines. The same for children—although the fonts might not need to be as large as it is for older adults—but children do need something larger and more spacious than most adults.

With my coyote novel, I used an eleven point Palatino Linotype font and a line spacing of seventeen points, which is larger than single line spacing, but less than one and a half line spacing. I figured the eleven-point font would be easy for young adults to read, and I made the line spacing a little bigger because I felt the single spacing was too crowded. (The line spacing of this paragraph is eighteen points in Word.)

With this manual that you are now reading, I felt it needed to be spacious, meaning I wanted a lot of white space to make it feel less intimidating. Technical manuals are hard enough to read without them being crowded. I also felt compelled to keep the page count as small as possible to keep the cost down. Moreover, I wanted to keep the word count down so I would have more room for the screen clips.

Try to create balance. Do not be afraid to have a lot of white space in your book, but try not to have it in big chunks (unless it is at the end of a chapter). This book has lots of white space between the lines and between paragraphs, as well as in the margins. The coyote novel also has quite of bit of white space between the lines.

When using artwork, such as clip art or your own art, take care in the placement of the graphic. In my coyote book, my first idea was to place a graphic at the beginning of each chapter. Each graphic would be two inches wide and on the right side of the first paragraph. The top of the graphic would be at the top of the first line of that paragraph. Not a bad

idea and I have seen books that did that. Then I had the idea of putting the graphic closer to the event it is illustrating and that is what I did.

Most of my graphics in my novel are two inches wide, but some are much wider, almost three and a half inches. I tried to vary where in the chapter I put the graphic, but I did placed them all next to the outer margin (I did not do this in this book), so they would be easier to see. Also I tried to balance the number of graphics on the left page roughly with the number that is on the right page. What you do in your book, if you decide to have graphics in it, is up to you. Whatever you do, make sure to take a moment to step back and ask yourself if there is a balance to it.

Let us go on to something else. In Word, PowerPoint and other programs, you can view your pages at different percentages. Remember 100% means you are viewing it at its actual size. I suggest you take a tape measure and measure the page at 100% to confirm this. Do this with Word, PowerPoint and any other program you are using.

I encourage you to experiment, but do not do it with your original manuscript. Copy part of it to a new Word file, give it a completely different name so it can never be confused with the original, and experiment with it. You will almost have to experiment with combinations of fonts, line spacing, margins, headers and footers, and graphics. In fact, just about everything you do to your book, you might want to experiment with first.

I also suggest you print many of these experiments to see how they will look in print. If you print one, remember there will be a difference between the size of your book when it is printed and the size of the printer paper. Your book may be 6 x 9, but the paper you are using at home is probably 8.5 x 11. Keep that in mind, then go ahead and print it.

The front and back matter

The front matter is all those pages that come before the first chapter. It can include a summary of your book, a title page, a copyright page, a dedication page, a quote or short story, and a table of contents. Your book does not have to include all of these pages, or any of them, or it can include other pages. To make your book look professional, it should probably have a title page and a copyright page. It may also need a few blank pages.

One long held tradition in book publishing is that the first page of the first chapter should be on the top of the paper that it is printed on. To put that a different way, that first page should be on the right side of the opened book. To see what I am talking about, open any professionally published book and the first page of the first chapter will be on the right side of the book, which is the top of the sheet of paper. In addition, any of the front material that is important, such as the title page or a dedication, should be the top of the paper. You may have to add a blank page to the front material to make this happen.

Pick out a handful of books and you will discover that most of them have a few blank pages included with the front material. If the page is important, you want it to be on the top of the sheet of paper—the right side of the book—because that is the more noticeable side. If you have to add a blank page to make that happen, then that is what you will have to do.

No law demands that you have anything before the first chapter. Even the copyright page, which might seem legally important, is not

necessary. Most books do have something occurring before the first chapter and the number of combinations is unlimited. Look at a selection of books and you will see different types of information put in the front material. I placed a one-page short story in my coyote novel. So if you feel the need to put something before chapter one, you can do it, just try to make it look good.

Just as your book can have front material, it can also have back material, such as indexes, biographies, suggested reading, notations, etc. If you decide to include them, you can look at other books for ideas how best to handle the back material. I have one important point about this. Most books do extend the page numbering to the back material, but if you do have any pages that are not part of the page numbering, you must still count those pages when calculating the width of the spine. Examples of back material that would not be part of the page count is an advertisement for another book you wrote or perhaps a crusade that you are promoting; neither is part of the main book and probably should not be part of the page count, but they do take up space and will make the book thicker.

Here is a table that shows how I arranged the front material of my coyote novel.

a. Front material for *The Song of the Coyote.*

Top of the page	Bottom of the page
Summary page	Blank page
Title page	Copyright page
Dedication page	Blank page
Short story	Blank page
Table of Contents (one page)	Blank page

Creating new pages

To create the different types of pages in your front material, you might have to add pages to the beginning of your manuscript. There are several types of page breaks, but we will use just two, a normal page break and a section page break.

a. Go to the very top of a page or the very bottom of a page.

b. Do **Ctrl-Enter**. This will create a page break and is the normal way to do it.

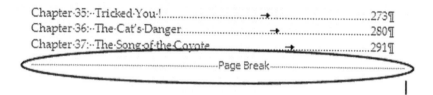

c. Sometimes it is important to separate the new page from what comes before it or after it, such as when they contain different formatting or different headers and footers. A sectional page break does this, and it tells Word that what comes before the section break and what comes after it will be treated differently. To do this, go to **Page Layout > Page Setup > Breaks > Section Break > Next Page**.

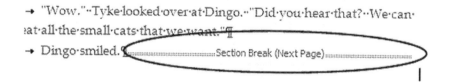

d. When working with page breaks and section page breaks, use the **Show/Hide** function. This will show you where the breaks are and

what kind they are. Also importantly, it will show you the paragraph marks. Go to **Home > Paragraph > Show/Hide**.

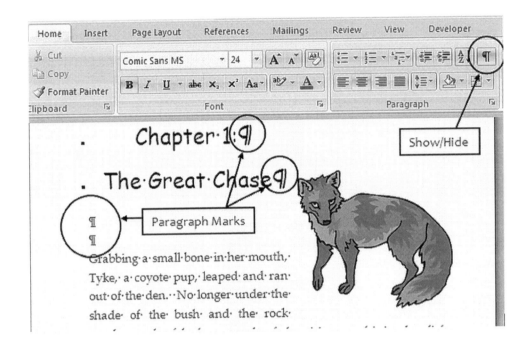

Summary Page

Create a blank page at the very top of the manuscript.

The summary page is a tool to frame the thinking of the reader and to create interest in your book. In some cases, it will be the first page that many people will see when they preview your book, but even if it is not, it can spark the interest of those who buy your book. If you decide to have one, make it as interesting as you can.

Type the name of the book and then type an interesting and enticing description of the book. In my coyote book, I used Comic Sans MS font for everything on this page and I bolded the whole page. I did this for emphasis, to make it jump out at the reader. My summary is 123 words; I would not have used bold and Comic Sans MS on anything more that.

The page under the summary should be a blank page.

Title Page

The title page is important and should be on the top of the sheet of paper. The title page is important, but it is interesting to ponder why. It may be obvious that your book needs a title page, but it has little information, usually the same information as the book cover. Most title pages will also have the publisher's name, but that could be put on the copyright page. So the title page is a little redundant, although most books have one.

How you design the title page is up to you. You can make it as artistic as you want. Most books have at a minimum the book's name, the author's name, the name of the illustrator—if the book has illustrations created just for it—and the name of the publishing company.

Place the name of the book at the top, then the author's name just under it. Centered it and make the book's name bigger than the author's name because the book is more important.

Experiment until you find the spacing between the book's name and the author's name and a font size that seems agreeable to what you want. Consider choosing a font already used in the book, perhaps the font used on the cover.

One thing I did with the coyote novel and this book was to put a graphic just below my name in the center of the page. For my coyote novel, I chose a graphic that I hoped would give the reader a feel for the novel. For this manual, I chose a graphic that I hope would make the book seem easy.

For the name of the publisher, I put "CreateSpace.com" at the bottom of the page. You do not have to do that, but it does look professional.

a. Font settings on the title page for *The Song of the Coyote*.

Title font > Palatino Linotype	Title font size > 22 pt
Author name font > Palatino Linotype	Author name font size > 14 pt
Publisher name font > Palatino Linotype	Publisher name font size > 12 pt
Graphic in center of page	

b. Font settings on the title page for this book:

First title font > Calibri	Title font size > 22 pt
Second title font > Calibri	Title font size > 18 pt
Author name font > Cambria	Author name font size > 14 pt
Publisher name font > Cambria	Publisher name font size > 13 pt
Graphic in center of page	

Copyright Page

Believe it or not, your book is copyrighted even if you do not use a copyright page. I do recommend that you have one anyway to remind people that it is indeed copyrighted. Some books after all are not copyrighted. Books that have been in circulation for a legal number of years lose their copyright status. Books by Mark Twain are an example of this.

Although the copyright page is important as a reminder to other people, it does not add to the artistic look of your book. For that reason, put it on the bottom side of the paper, which is the left side of the book. I placed the copyright page behind the title page. It is commonplace to put the copyright page here and makes me wonder if the purpose of the title page is simply to hide the copyright page.

If you look at most published books, the copyright information is understated, perhaps in a small font and certainly not bolded. This is a good idea because you want to diminish how easily noticeable the copyright information is, after all it does not make your book more artistic.

From my research, and I am not a lawyer, you need to have at least several things on your copyright page: the word "Copyright," the symbol "©," the date of the year and the author's name. Something like this: "Copyright © 2007 by Jimmy Clay" or like "Copyright © 2007 by Jimmy Clay and its licensors."

Next you need something more specific to point out all the things that are copyrighted in your book. In truth, you do not have to put anything here because everything is copyrighted; at least that is my understanding. But it is good to remind people. You might want a statement that is something like this: "All rights reserved. No part of this book can be reproduced or used for any reason or by anyone without permission. The only exception being small excerpts from this book which will be used to glorify and promote it."

You can use that statement if you want. If you look at other books, you will notice that the wording changes depending on the publisher. There is no set legal wording that you must adhere to. Do not copy someone else's wording, word for word, although it is okay to get ideas from them.

If you use clip art give credit to the clip art companies and be sure you have the right to use the clip art. If someone is drawing your art for you, give them credit too.

The copyright page is a good place to stick any other information that you feel the need to express, but do not know where to put. In my coyote novel, I thanked my sister and niece for reading the book and catching some errors. I also gave my web address. In addition, I stuck in information about another book I wrote and published.

Dedication Page

Many books do not have a dedication page, so if you have no one to dedicate your book to, do not get stressed out about it. On the other hand, it is an easy way to score a few points.

In my coyote novel, I dedicated my book to my mom and dad. This made sense because two of the main characters in the book are Tyke's mom and dad, who are referred to simply as "mom and dad." It seemed artistic to make this dedication. Also the company I work for is having financial problems, so I might need to live with my mom and dad, so scoring a few points is in order.

I added a graphic of paw prints. I thought it was a nice touch.

The dedication page should be on the top of the sheet of paper it is on, which is the right side of the book. If you are going to the trouble of dedicating the book to someone, you want to put the dedication in a position of honor, which is the top of the sheet of paper that it is printed.

The bottom of that sheet of paper is usually blank. You should have the dedication page on the top and a blank page on the bottom.

Short story or quote

The first book I had published, *Founding Father: The Life and Times of John Neely Bryan*, I used a quote I had found on the Internet, which I felt summed up the life of the character.

In my coyote novel, I wrote a short, short story. I am not sure that this one-page story sums up the novel, but it does give the flavor. This, I hope, will help generate interest in story. Someone thinking about buying the book cannot read the whole book, but they can read the short story.

This page goes on the top of the paper and a blank page on the bottom.

Table of Contents

The table of contents can also be a quick way to generate interest if you give the chapters interesting names. When I am sizing up a book, trying to decide whether I want to buy it, the first place I look is the table of contents. If the chapters sound interesting, that is a good way to get me to buy it. The table of contents is one of the items that Amazon will allow the customer to preview, so it is important to make your chapters sound interesting.

The table of contents can also have a title. You can use the words "Table of Contents" or just "Contents." This book is an example of a book with a table of contents that does not have a title.

Microsoft Word can generate the table of contents for you. To do this, you have to create the chapter titles using a heading style.

a. To create a table of contents, first create a blank page, then go to **References > Table of Contents > Table of Contents**

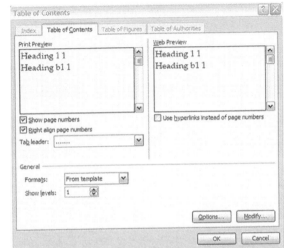

b. Go to the very bottom and click **Insert Table of Contents**.

c. A dialogue box will pop up. First, uncheck **use hyperlinks instead of page numbers**.

d. Under **Show levels** select the number of headings levels you want to use for your table of contents. The chapter titles in my novel use just one level (but two styles, both styles are based on the **Heading 1** style), for your book you may want to use several levels, especially if it is nonfiction. The sublevels must also have a header style, such as Heading 2, Heading 3....

e. Make sure **Show page numbers** and **Right align page numbers** are checked.

f. Choose a tab leader and choose a format.

g. Click **Okay**.

h. To create my chapter titles I used two styles, one for the top line and one for the bottom (I will tell you why later). Word picked up both styles when generating the table of contents. To get the table of contents correct, I had to edit it, which can be done, but I had to do some experimenting to get it right.

i. Next, highlight the entire table of contents, then choose a font and point size. The font of my content page is Palatino Linotype. To limit my content page to just one page, I changed the font size to nine points, which is small.

j. Try to start your table of contents on the top page of the paper, although I have found some professional books that did not do this. If your table of content is long, it is okay to let it flow to the back page. Many books have a table of contents that are two, three, four pages or more. If your book is one of these, there should be no blank pages between these pages; they should be continuous. There is no need for any blank pages at the end of the table of contents, unless one is needed for the reason stated next.

First page of the first chapter

The first page of the first chapter will probably be next, right after the table of contents.

This page should be on the right side of the book. It should be on the top side of the paper, never on the bottom side. It should be on the top because it is the beginning of your book. This is a kind of drum roll to get the book started. The other chapters that follow can start on the top or bottom of the paper.

If necessary, add blank pages to the front material to make sure this page is on top. So for example, if the last page of your table of contents ended on the top page of a sheet of paper, the bottom of that sheet should be a blank page, and the next page, which will be the top page of the next sheet of paper, will be the first page of the first chapter.

Embedding fonts

If you store your manuscript on a USB stick and work on it using a different computer, you probably need to embed your fonts, which means the fonts you use are put into your manuscript. Then your manuscript will not depend on the host computer having the font on it. If you are using a font that is not common, this is even more important.

a. To embed the fonts go to **Office Button > Word Options > Save** and go down to where it says **Preserve fidelity when shaving this document**. Make sure you select the correct manuscript.

b. Check the box next to **Embed fonts in the file**.

c. Click **Okay**.

Document paper size

The manuscript paper size is easy to change. While you are writing your book, you can keep your manuscript size at the default 8.5 x 11. When you finish writing and start preparing the book for publishing, the first thing to do is to change this to the size you chose for your book. Do this before you add any graphics.

a. Go to **Page Layout > Page Setup > Size > More Paper Sizes**.

b. Go to the very top where it says **Paper Size**. Enter the size you want your book to be. Remember you cannot put just any size down. Your choice of size must be one of the sizes allowed by CreateSpace. Check their website for the current list of sizes they allow.

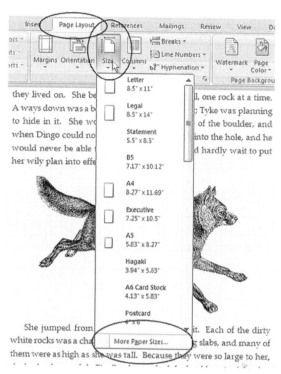

c. Be sure to use the correct boxes. Do not invert the width and the height.

d. Go to **Apply to** box at the bottom of the dialogue box and select **Whole document**.

e. Click the **Okay** button.

f. Settings for *The Song of the Coyote.*

Width > 6 (inches)	Height > 8

g. Settings for this book.

Width > 8	Height > 10

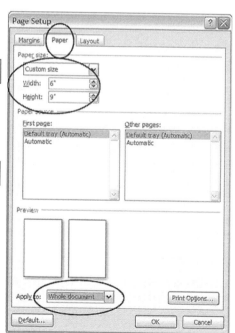

Margins and line spacing

Margins are easy enough. It is a good idea to use a different margin size for the inside part of the book than is

used for the outside part of the book. Because the inside margin is used for the binding of the book, making it a little larger than the outside margin gives the inside a little extra room for the binding. This may not be necessary if your book has large margins, such as this book; but my coyote novel has small margins, so I made the inner margin a little bigger. To have inner and outer margins of different sizes, use the **mirrored margins** option.

That is easy, but here is the hard part (this may be confusing). On your computer, the first page and second page are shown as individual pages. However, in your book, the second page will be wrapped to the back of the first page (they will be sharing the same piece of paper). So looking at the pages on your computer, on page one the inside margin is to the left side of the page. On page two, the inside margin is on the right side. This is confusing if you have never given it any thought. The best way to clarify this will be for you to print the first two pages of your book. Then place the two pages facing you, as they would be positioned on your computer and put a mark on the left margin of each. Then slide the second page to the back of the first, as it would be if it were printed in a book. Notice that on the front page, the mark is still on the left side (the inner margin), but on the back it is now on the right side (the outer margin).

If you are creating your inside and outside margins with different sizes, you have to use Word's **mirror margin** function so Word will know what you are trying to do. If the differences in the sizes of the inside and outside margins are large enough, you might see—while using your computer—the margins flip flopping back and forth when you scroll down your manuscript. This is not a problem, but if you are not aware of what is happening, you might think it is. One thing about the mirror margin function is that it is much easier to use than it is to explain. So take heart.

Finally, about the line spacing. You might think you must use single space, one and a half space, or double space for the line spacing, but you do not. Word gives you the freedom to go anywhere in between. I think this is a good thing. If the page layout feels crowded, making the spacing between the lines a little bigger, but not much bigger, can make a difference in the way the book feels. I did this with my coyote novel.

Setting the margins

A smaller margin can help you save pages if you have a wordy book. A large margin can increase pages if you have a not so wordy book. A large margin makes a book feel more relaxed. A small margin will make it more intense. If a margin is large enough, you can put stuff in it like text boxes and graphics.

a. Go to **Page Layout > Page Setup > Small arrow > Margins**.

b. At the bottom of the dialogue box, where it says **Apply to** select **Whole Document**.

c. The size you set your margins is subject to experimentation. I would try different settings to see

what you are comfortable with. Unless you have large margins going all the way around, I suggest you select **mirror margins** in the section that says **Pages**. Make the inner margin a little bigger than the outer margin to provide room for the binding of the book.

d. Under orientation, most books use **portrait**.

e. Page Layout settings for *The Song of the Coyote*.

Top Margin > 1	Bottom Margin > 1
Inside Margin > 0.75	Outside Margin > 0.5
Page Orientation > Portrait	
Pages > Multiple Pages > Mirror margins	

f. Settings for this book.

Top Margin > 1.25	Bottom Margin > 1.00
Left Margin > 1.25	Right Margin > 1.25
Page Orientation > Portrait	
Pages > Multiple Pages > Normal	

Fonts

The creation of fonts is an artistic endeavor. I never gave this any thought until I researched this book. It turns out that there are entire web pages devoted to specific fonts with credit given to the font's creator. Different fonts can have very different designs. Some fonts are bigger that other fonts, though they may claim to have the same point size. Some fonts are darker than others. Some fonts are loopy and some are blockish. Some fonts are highly regarded and some fonts—such as the Comic Sans MS font—have websites dedicated to eliminating them; imagine a font that has its own hate community.

Not only does each font have its own name, each font is a type. There are types of fonts, and there are types within types. There are also traditions with regard to how fonts are used. I do not know if those traditions are valid, but people are used to seeing fonts used in a certain way, so think twice before bucking those trends. Go along, to get along, right? If you do buck the trend, I am sure there are font connoisseurs who will notice and complain.

Anyway, there are two major types of fonts that we are going to worry about. If there are more major types out there, I do not want to know about them, and we will not worry about subtypes. I am going to tell you about serif fonts and sans serif fonts. The thing to remember about these types of fonts is that serif fonts have something sans serif fonts do not have; in fact, the "san" in "sans serif" comes from the French "sans" which means without. One more thing, the words you are now reading are formed with a serif font called Cambria.

What is so special about serif fonts? Well, it is a small thing. It is the little bars at the end of many of the letters that makes a serif a serif. It is the lack of those bars that make a sans serif, not a serif. Find a "p" somewhere in this paragraph, and look at the ends of that "p." The little cap at the top and bottom of the "p" is the serif. You will see this with the "Y" too. The "T" is another good example. You should get the ideal (take a look at the "l").

Now take a look at this paragraph. The font of this paragraph is called Calibri sans serif. Try to find a "p," "Y," "T," and "l," and observe the difference between them and those letters in the previous paragraph. The difference is that these fonts, the fonts in this paragraph, lack serifs.

Okay, those are the two major schools of fonts. If you do a study of these schools, you may read about subdivisions of these types, but we will not worry about those here. More important is why this matters. This matters because your book needs contrasting fonts. One of the traditions of fontology is that fonts need to be contrasted with each other. To put it simply, use one type of font for your titles and another type for the body.

Here is another cherished tradition in font lore. Use serif fonts for body text and sans serif for titles. The rationality of this is that the serif, the little piece at the end of the letters, leads the eye to the next letter. To me this sounds like a job for the MythBusters. Regardless, that is the tradition, and who does not love tradition? One less thing to think about. I should briefly mention the exception to this tradition. If you are preparing a website, just to confuse us, the tradition on websites is that sans serif fonts are used for both the titles and the body.

In this book, I used Calibri for the titles and Cambria for the body.

You might also want to consider using different fonts for text boxes and lists if your book uses those, one type for the text box and one type for the list. I have noticed that some books will use a sans serif font for lists and text boxes. This might help the reader, because the reader will more easily see that something has changed, just in case he is not paying attention to what he is reading. Another point is that it makes your book look less boring, less monolithic, and adds emphasis. I did not do this for this book because I used so many lists they are just a normal part of the book.

So use different fonts, but do not overdo it. Do not give your reader a headache. Remember, some is good, but less is more.

Finally, I suggest that you experiment with different font combinations. Try using different fonts for the title and see how they look when combined with different body fonts (and different fonts for text boxes and lists). I suggest printing them and writing on each printout the name of the fonts and the point size. Then compare the different printouts and find a combination that feels right. I found that some fonts seemed business like, while others seemed easy going. I used Palatino Linotype in my coyote novel because it seems more laid back and relaxed.

Fonts can be expensive, so unless you understand them better than I do and you know what you want, I would stick with the ones that come with Windows and Word.

Change the normal style

What are styles? A style is a set of formatting that has a name. For example, if you want all your paragraphs to have a Cambria font at thirteen points, eighteen point spacing between each line, a twelve point space between each paragraph, and be justified; instead of manually setting that formatting for each paragraph, you can create a style. That is basically what I did for this book. I set the normal style to have those settings.

The normal style is the default style for a Word manuscript. In fact many of the other styles in a manuscript are based on the normal style. A style based on it will have all the settings of the normal style, except for the exceptions that you select. To make changes to the normal style:

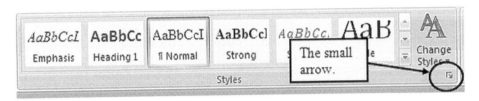

a. Go to **Home > Styles > Small arrow**.

b. Click the black mark on the right side of the normal style and choose **modify** on the small menu that will pop up. This will bring up the **Modify Style** dialogue box.

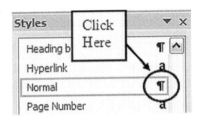

c. At the bottom left of this dialogue box, go to **Format > paragraph**. This will bring up the paragraph dialogue box. Select the settings you want your book to have. When you finish, click **Okay**.

d. Paragraph settings for the normal style of *The Song of the Coyote*.

Alignment > Justified	
Indentation:	
Left > 0	Special > none
Right > 0	
Spacing	
Before > 0	Line Spacing
After > 0	Exactly > 17 pt

e. Paragraph settings for the normal style of this book.

Alignment > Justified	
Indentation:	
Left > 0	Special > none
Right > 0	
Spacing	
Before > 0	Line Spacing
After > 12 pt	Exactly > 18 pt

f. Just as a note: When I wrote *The Song of the Coyote*, many years ago, I used the tab key to indent each paragraph. If you have not written your book yet, I suggest that under Indentation you set the **Special** setting to **First Line** and the **By** setting to 0.25. Now each time you start a new paragraph, Word will indent the paragraph for you.

g. Next you will need to create the font settings for

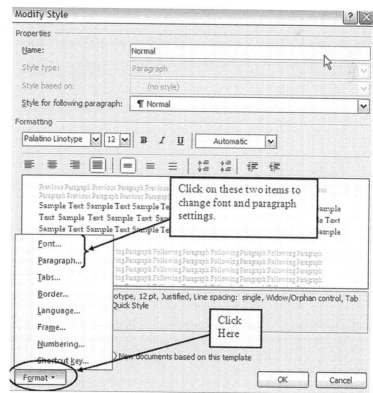

your normal style.

h. You should still be in the **Modify Style** dialogue box. Go to **Format > font.** Select your fonts and then click **Okay.**

i. Font settings for the normal style of *The Song of the Coyote.*

Font > Palatino Linotype	Font Style > Regular
Font Size > 11 pt	Color > Automatic

j. Font settings for the normal style of this book.

Font > Cambria	Font Style > Regular
Font Size > 13 pt	Color > Automatic

k. If you have finished, click **Okay** again to see the changes in your manuscript.

l. Did the changes to the normal style change your manuscript as planned?

m. If changing the normal style did not change your paragraphs, check that your paragraphs are based on the normal style. If not, click on the paragraph and see which style becomes highlighted in the styles dialogue box.

n. Make your format changes to that style.

Chapter titles

Some books do not have chapter titles, although I believe they can build interest in your book. Deciding how you want the beginning of each chapter to look is something you will have to experiment with. I am going to give you instructions on how I did it with my coyote novel.

Because I feel it looks better, the chapter number and the chapter name will be on different lines, with the chapter name a line below the chapter number.

Both lines of the chapter title need the same font and point size, which needs to be different than the font and point size of the body text. This will provide some contrast between the way the title looks and the body text looks.

The title needs its own small area above the body text. The goal is to make the title easy to read and to give a clear indication that a new chapter is starting.

What I am going to say now is difficult to explain, but will become clearer when we create the headers. Each of the title lines, the chapter number and the chapter name, need different header styles—such as "**Heading 1**" for the chapter number and "**Heading b1**" for the chapter name. Here is the hard to understand part, they will have different styles but those styles will be exact copies of each other. I will not try to explain this here, too hard, but it will be clearer after we make the headers.

By default, you should already have a **Heading 1** style. Highlight the first line of your title and give it the **Heading 1** style.

Chances are the default settings for the **Heading 1** styles are not what you want. Go into it, just as we did with the Normal style and change the sittings until the first line of the title looks as you want it to.

Heading 1 style settings for *The Song of the Coyote*.

Paragraph:	
Alignment > centered	
Indentation:	
Left > 0	Special > none
Right > 0	
Spacing	
Before > o	Line spacing > single
After > 12 pt	
Font:	
Font > Comic Sans MS	Font Style > Regular
Size > 20 pt	
Font Color > Automatic	

a. Next we need to create the **Heading b1** style. This is very easy to do.

b. Go to **Home > Styles > small arrow**.

c. A dialogue box will pop up. At the very bottom, left side of it is a button that will say **New** if the cursor is hovered over it. Click that button.

d. You have to do two things here. Where it says **Name** give it the name "**Heading b1.**" Then, a few lines down where it says **style based on**, select "**Heading 1.**"

Click **Okay**, and that is it. The **Heading b1** style will be exactly like the **Heading 1** style, and that will help us later when creating the headers at the top of the pages.

e. Now all you have to do is go to each chapter in your book, make sure the chapter number is on the top line and the chapter name is on the bottom. Then apply the **Heading 1** style to the chapter number and the **Heading b1** style to the chapter name.

f. While you are doing this, there is one other thing you might want to do. Check to make sure all the chapter titles have the same spacing. In my coyote novel, I placed one line above the title (just by tapping the enter key) and two lines below the title. Put another way, my novel has one line space between the title and the top margin, and two line spaces between the title and the body text.

g. One more thing, the first paragraph of each chapter is not supposed to be indented. This is a good time to make sure yours are not. In fact if the chapter has subheadings, you probably should not indent the first paragraph after those subheadings either.

Headers and footers

Do you like headers and footers? They are nice, but a pain to set up. You would not think so, because they seem easy enough, but speaking for myself, I have had problems every time I messed with them. My advice here is that you expect some problems. I am not talking about hard to understand and figure out kinds of problems. I am talking about discipline, getting the header and footer to behave. My goal is to make this easy for you, but after writing these steps, I still have problems with them. Perhaps, what I am talking about will become

clearer when you do them. If it does, do not get frustrated. Take a break if you need to. Better yet, try to get in a good eight hours of sleep.

We are going to do several things with the headers and footers. With headers, we are going to suppress the header in the front material and on the first page of each chapter. In addition, we are going to have different headers for even and odd pages. The even page will have the number and name of the chapter, and the odd page will have the name of the book.

In the footers, we are going to have page numbers. This does not seem like it would be any problem, but you will want the page numbers to start with chapter one, not with the material before chapter one. You want the page numbers to run continuously from chapter to chapter. This is not hard, but you have to know how to do it. You will have to be watchful and ready to crack the whip of discipline, because the footer will want to number the front material also, and you do not want that.

Headers and page numbers

Life does not begin until you have dealt with headers and page numbers in Word. It is not that hard, but it is frustrating. Experience should make it better, but it does not. I am not telling you this to scare you, just to warn you. You can do this, but you may need a soundproof room where you can go and scream. Check and double check to make sure your headers and page numbers are doing what you told them to do. Once you have gotten them to do it, do not just assume they will continue to do it.

a. Before we start doing the headers and page numbers, we will need to set some of Word's options. Go to **Page Layout > Page Setup > small arrow**.

b. There are three tabs at the top, click the **Layout** tab.

c. Go to the bottom of the dialogue box and where it says **Apply to** select **Whole document**.

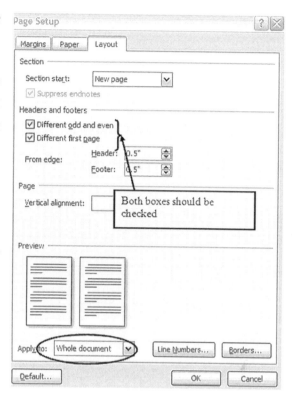

d. Towards the top of the dialogue box, under the section that says **Headers and footers**, select both of the boxes. The box for **Different odd and even** should be selected and the box for **Different first page** should also be selected.

e. The **Different odd and even** setting will allow us to have the book title on the odd page and the chapter title on the even page. The **Different first page** setting will let us have no header on the first page of each chapter.

f. Go to the first page of the first chapter. There should be a **section break** between it and the front material. A **section break** is not the same as the break created when using the **ctrl-enter** keys.

g. First click the **Show/hide** button so you can see what is going on. Go to **Home > Paragraph > Show/Hide Button**.

h. Look at the page just before the first chapter; does it say **Page Break** or **Section Break** or perhaps nothing? It needs to say

Section Break (Next Page). (To get comfortable doing this you might need to experiment on another document.)

i.   If it says **Page Break,** click the **Page Break** and delete it. Then go to **Page Layout > Page Setup > Breaks > Sections > Next Page**. This will create a section that will wall off the front material from the main body of the book, but remember that it is a short wall with a door, so we will have to be careful with it.

j.   If you have never done this, this might be a little tricky, but work at it. Remember that you want chapter one to start at the top of the next sheet of paper after the section break. If there is a blank page before chapter one, there should only be one blank page and it should contain the section break.

k.   Next you need to do this at the end of each chapter. The chapters need also to be separated by a section break, not a page break. Go through your entire book and make sure there is a section break at the end of each chapter. (This will prevent the headers from appearing on the title page of the chapters.) Also make sure there are no blank pages between the chapters.

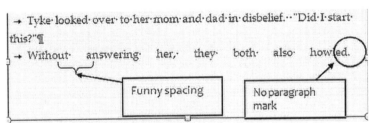

l.   One more worry, make sure you do not delete the paragraph mark of the very last paragraph of the chapters. If you do delete this ending paragraph mark, it will create a funny spacing of the words, assuming you have paragraph justification turned on.

m. Now for the fun part, we can start to create the header. Go to your chapter one and click on the second page of the chapter (not the first). On the second page, go to **Insert > Header & Footer > Header > Edit Header**. Like magic, this will take you to the header of the page and the header ribbon will open.

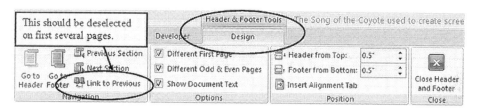

n. The _very_ first thing you will want to do is to <u>unselect</u> the **Link to Previous** button. I have talked about some of the problems I have had with creating headers; not unselecting this button causes most of them. You do not want your headers going up into the front material, and if you do not unselect this setting, they will. So if you forget to unselect it when you first create your headers, you will need to unselect it, and then you will have to delete all the headings from the front material. Also do not assume the **Link to Previous** button will stay unselected.

o. On this page, page two, you want the name of the chapter. To do this, go to **Insert > Text > Quick Parts > Field**. On the left side of the dialogue box that opens, scroll down to **StyleRef** and highlight it. On the right side highlight **Heading 1**, then click **Okay**. Then create two spaces by tapping the space bar twice. Then go to **Insert > Text > Quick Parts > Field**. Next do the same thing as above, scroll down to **StyleRef**, but this time select **Heading b1**, and click **Okay**. If you had used **Heading 1** for both the upper and lower title lines of the chapter title, only one of those title lines could appear in the header.

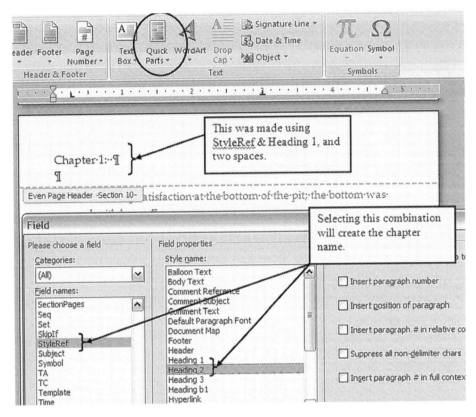

p. Now highlight this header and choose a font and font size for it.

q. Now your even pages will have the name of the chapter on it. Next click on page three. Go to **Insert > Header & Footer > Header > Edit Header**. Be _very_ sure to <u>unselect</u> **Link to Previous**. Now just type the name of the book, and give it the same font and size as the previous header.

r. Go back to the front material and make sure there are no headers in it. If there are, delete them. If deleting the headers in the front material causes the headers in the main body to disappear, you will have to repeat this process, making sure the **Link to Previous** is unselected, and make sure there is a **section break** separating the first chapter from the front material.

s.   Now go to each chapter and make sure there are no headers on the title pages (the title page of the chapter is the first page of the chapter). If there are, make sure there is a section break between that chapter and the previous chapter. Then double click the header on the chapter's title page and delete it. Make sure deleting this header does not delete all the headers; if it does, start over.

t.   No sweat.

u.   The font settings for headers in *The Song of the Coyote.*

Font > Comic Sans MS	Font size > 12 pt

v.   The font settings for headers in this book

Font > Calibri	Font size > 16 pt

Page numbers

Word 2007 comes with many preset styles for page numbers. To save yourself extra work, I would use one of them. The one I chose for my coyote novel is the **Tildes center, bottom.**

a.   Click on the first page of the first chapter.

b.   Go to **Insert > Header & Footer > Page Number > Bottom of page.** Choose a style. The **Header & Footer Ribbon** will open.

c. The *very*, very first thing to do after selecting the page number style is to unselect **Link to Previous**.

d. If you wish to change the font and size of the page number, you can do so by highlighting the page number in the footer and then selecting a font and font size.

e. Go to page two and do the same thing, making sure to unselect **Link to Previous**.

f. Go to page three and do this again. (I always had to do this to the first three pages. I do not know why.)

g. The font and size used for the page number in *The Song of the Coyote*.

Font > Palatino Linotype	Font size > 12 pt

h. The font and size used for the page number in this book.

Font > Cambria	Font size > 13 pt

i. Now go up to the front material and make sure they do not have page numbers; if they do, you will have to delete those page numbers. To delete the page number, open the footer by clicking quickly on the offending page number several times. Then highlight and delete them. Now make sure you still have page numbers in the main body of your book.

j. If you do not, repeat the steps, unselect **Link to Previous**. Check that there is a section break between the front material and the first chapter.

k. If you have created page numbers in the main body of your book, without doing so in the front material, you have done well. Now go to chapter two. Do the page numbers start over, beginning at one? If so, click on the first page of that chapter. Go to **Insert > Header & Footer > Page Numbers > Format Page Numbers**. A dialogue box will pop up; select the button in front of **Continue from previous section**. You will have to do this for every chapter.

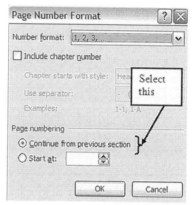

l. Next, are the page numbers too close to the body text? To move the page numbers down, go to **Insert > Header & Footer > Footer > Edit Footer**.

m. On the ribbon bar that opens up, go to **Header & Footer Tools > Position**. Where it says **Footer from Bottom,** change the settings until the page number is far enough from the text. Check every chapter to make sure this change is the same for each of them.

Graphics in general

Graphics are fun, but they are also a lot of work. If you can draw or know someone who wants to draw for you, you will have the best type

of graphics for your book. You will have to scan your drawings and get them into your computer. My advice is that you draw your picture bigger than you will need it. If you do this, you can reduce the picture in size with no loss of quality, but if you draw it too small and decide later that you want it bigger, you will lose quality. By drawing it bigger than you need it, you will have more options. After it is drawn, scan it at 300 DPI, but no more and no less because that is what you need.

I cannot draw, so all the art in my novel and this book are either clip art or screen clips. If you are not using your own drawings, I would recommend you buy several clip art packages (make sure they are royalty free). You will discover that the clip art packages are different, not only with the clip art they have but also with the program they give you to retrieve the clip art.

I do not know much about graphics, and what I do know I learned while preparing my coyote novel and this manual. You may know more than I do. My goal here is to help you get going, not to be the expert and do it all for you. That is what I will do.

In my coyote novel and this book, each graphic was specially prepared, and you should do the same for your book. Before inserting a graphic in the book, make sure it is set at 300 DPI, that the size of the graphic when view at 100% (not zoomed in or zoomed out) is the size it needs to be in the book, that the graphic is gray scaled, and that the graphic is in the TIFF format. Then insert the graphic into the Word manuscript, do not copy and paste it.

Some people might ask, why? Why can I not just copy and paste the graphic into Word then resize it using the handlebars that Word provides? Why do I have to use the TIFF format? Well, you do not have to use TIFF, and I am willing to admit there might be better ways of doing this. If you think you know enough about graphics to do it on your own, please give it a try. In fact in my coyote novel, I used a PNG graphic for the cover clip art because the art did not work well in TIFF format (the colors became translucent in the PDF file). Because much of the advice I am giving is advice I found researching on the Internet, I am not claiming to be an expert. I do encourage you to take extra care in preparing the graphics. Remember that graphics are extra elements that sit inside your manuscript that the commercial printer will have to read. If you fiddle with the graphic by resizing it with the handle bars, you are running the risk of confusing the printer, and the graphic might print as a black blob.

I believe it is best to put the graphic into the manuscript as you want the graphic to be, and not use the tools Word provides to change the graphic in any way. The exception to this will be making the graphics background transparent. We will use the Word and PowerPoint transparency wand for that. I did this with my coyote novel and it does work.

Do you have to use the TIFF graphic format? No you do not, but I found TIFF was highly recommended as a format when I was doing my research, so that is the format I decided to use. If you have a favorite format and want to use it, there is nothing wrong with trying it. You may want to experiment. I do know, from my research, that different types of graphics are good for different things. Some are best for the web, while others are better for print. Try printing a graphic in different formats to see what, if any, differences there are. Use the highest quality print setting on your printer (so you can see, as best as possible, what they would look like on a commercial printer). In addition to the cover of my coyote novel, I also had to use the PNG format for several graphics on the cover of this book—the man at the

desk, the printing press, and three howling coyotes (this refers to the first edition of this book, which used PowerPoint to make the cover). For those graphics, using the PNG format made setting the transparent background easier. If you are having trouble getting a graphic to work, do try saving the graphic in a different format.

There are two general types of graphics. There are raster (also called bitmap) graphics that are made of dots and there are vector graphics that are made of lines and mathematic equations. I used only raster graphics in the manuscript and cover. But vector clip art are useful because you can make them larger without loss of quality, then reformatted them as a raster graphic and use in your book. The clip art programs come with different types of graphics. The clip art in The Big Box of Art 410,000 was all vector graphics.

Resizing raster graphics is no problem if you are making them smaller. Think twice about making them bigger. If you do make them bigger, you will lose quality. That does not mean you cannot do it, many of the screen clips in this book were made larger. The trick here, if you are going to make a raster graphic bigger, is to use a good resample filter. A resample filter is a small utility that fills in the gaps created when you stretch a graphic to make it bigger. Some resample filters do a better job than others; always use the slowest resample filter. The reason I chose to use IrfanView is because it does a much better job at this than the other programs I experimented with. The difference is noticeable.

Installing graphics

I placed many graphics in my novel and in this book. I encourage you to put them in your book too. Graphics are nice, fun, and create eye relief. If you cannot draw, you will have to do what I did and buy clip art.

We already talked about the requirements for the graphics. I will just repeat them here. If you are creating a black and white book, the graphics must be gray scaled. The size of the graphic, when viewed at 100%, must be the size it will be in the book (do not adjust your graphic with the handles in Word). The graphic must be set at 300 DPI. Moreover, the graphic must be inserted into the manuscript, not pasted. Unless you have a reason not to, use the TIFF graphic format.

All clip art packages are different. Many of them come with vector clip art, which is useful because they can be increased or reduced without worrying about loss of quality.  However, raster clip art are made of dots and are not scalable. You can make clip art made of dots smaller without loss of quality, but if you try to increase their size, quality will be loss. This is similar to taking a small resolution photo (also made of dots) and trying to enlarge it; it gets gritty.

As much as possible use the tools provided by the clip art package to change the size of the clip art and the DPI. Some clip art packages will let you set the size, but not the DPI. My advice here is to set the size to a large one, then copy the clip art in IrfanView and set the DPI to three hundred, then set the size to fit the book, and save it as a TIFF.

To help you get started, I will work through one clip art and one screen clip. The clip art to the right is an illustration of three of the coyote pups in the novel. They love to play and Tyke, the star of the novel, has

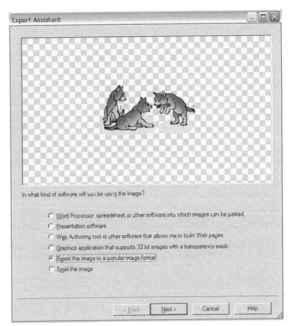

to learn to take care of them. I found this clip art using The Big Box of Art 410,000.

a. Installing the graphics should be the last thing you do to prepare the internal material. Do everything in this book above this section before trying to install any graphics. Word is not the best at handling graphics. They tend to jump around. For example, if you try to change the margins after putting the graphics in, you may have to go back and reposition all the graphics again.

b. Double click on the clip art and The Big Box of Art pulls up the first of a series of dialogue boxes. The dialogue boxes will help you to export the art in almost any format and size that you want.

c. Choose **Export the image to a popular image format**. Click **Next**, change the size and select 300 DPI. Click **Next** again; you probably can leave this next page alone. Again click **Next**; choose **TIFF with transparency**. Then browse to the directory where you want the clip art to be exported. Then click the **Export** button and it will be saved to the hard drive.

d. Open IrfanView, which is a graphic viewer. In IrfanView, go **File > Open,** and browse to the directory where you saved the clip art.

e. This clip art is already set to the required size and at 300 DPI. The next thing to do is convert it to grayscale. This not only sets it to the black and white format, but also reduces the size of the clip art. Go to **Image > Covert to Grayscale**.

f. Not all clip art (and screen clips) are as easily prepared as the art in The Big Box of Art. You can use IrfanView to set the DPI and the size of the graphic. If you have a graphic that is not set at 300 DPI and is not the size you need, open the graphic in IrfanView. Go to **Image > Resize/Resample**. This will pull up a dialogue box.

g. To the right, where it says **Size method:** select **Resample (better quality)** and choose the **Lanczos filter**.

h. At the bottom, where it says **DPI**, change that number to 300.

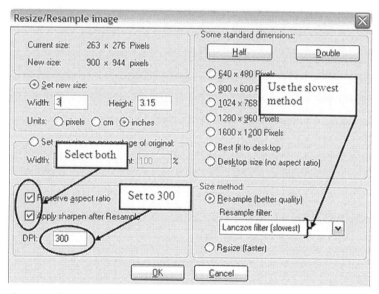

i. Right above that, make sure the two boxes are checked, especially the one that says **Preserve aspect ratio**.

j. Above, where it says **New Size**, change the units to inches. Then change the width to what you want, the height will change automatically.

k. Click **Okay**.

l. You will notice, after making these changes, that the clip art you view in IrfanView is probably not the size you specified. IrfanView, and other graphic viewers, does not use inches to measure graphics, it use dots or pixels. For example, this graphic's DPI was set to three hundred, and let us assume that it is 3 x 3.15. Doing some math, 3 inches x 300 dots = 900 dots wide, and 3.15 in x 300 dots = 945 dots high. That is what you are seeing when using IrfanView, you are seeing every dot, 900 dots (or pixels) wide and 945 dots (or pixels) high. This might appear strange, it does to me, but that is just the way many graphic viewers do it. When the graphic is inserted in Word, it will be 3 x 3.15 when viewed at 100%.

m. Next save the graphic as a TIFF file. In IrfanView, go to **File > Save as**. First, check the box where is says **Show options dialog**, at the very bottom. Then where it says **Save as type** choose TIF. A box will pop up to the right that says **TIFF save options**. The only thing selected should be the one that says **None**. Now give your file a name, find the directory where you want it saved, and save it. Do not try to copy it from IrfanView straight into Word. Word will convert the file and you may lose some of the settings.

n. Now open your Word manuscript and click where you want your image to be. To insert the image, go to **Insert > Illustrations > Picture** and browse to where you saved your clip art. Double click the clip art and it should pull up in Word.

o. When it pulls up in Word, it may do something funny. When I do this, all I see is the box with no graphic. You should see the **Picture Tools Format Ribbon**. Go to **Picture Tools Format > Arrange > Text Wrapping** and select **More Layout Options**. Select **Square** or

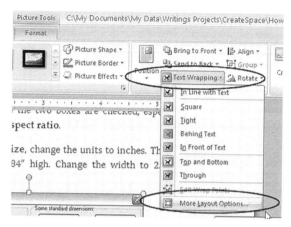

Top and Bottom. Enter 0.13 for all the boxes in **Distance from text**. You should now see the image. Notice it is the size that you set in IrfanView.

p. Drag and position the image to where you want it to be. **But:**

q. **Do <u>NOT</u> save your manuscript! ! !**

r. Before saving the manuscript, the compression settings have to be changed. If they are not changed, Word might reduce the DPI settings of the graphic when you save it, which would be bad.

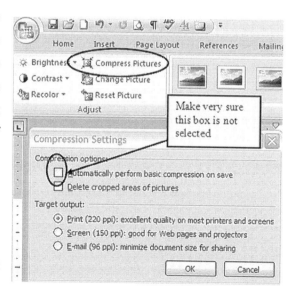

s. Double click the clip art to select it and to bring up the **Picture Tools Format Ribbon**. Go to **Picture Tools Format > Adjust > Compress Picture**. Do **_not_** click the **Okay**

button; instead, click **Options**. Make sure the two boxes are unchecked under **Compression Options**, especially the box for **Automatically perform basic compression on save**. You do **<u>NOT</u>** want this button selected.

t. Uncheck those boxes and click **Okay**. Then click **Cancel** on the next dialogue box. Then you might want to redo this process to make sure those boxes are not checked. The good news is that you only have to do this once per manuscript, not for every graphic you insert.

u. The next chore is to set the graphic's background to transparent. This is not hard. Double click the graphic to select it and bring up the **Picture Tools Format Ribbon**. Go to **Picture Tools Format > Adjust > Recolor**. Then click at the bottom where it says **Set Transparent Color**. You will see the cursor turn into a wand. Position the wand over the graphic's background that you would like to be able to see through and click on the background.

v. That should do it. To test that the background is transparent, go to **Page Layout > Page Background > Page Color**. Hover the curser over the colors and the color of your manuscript should change. You should be able to see this change of color through the graphic's background.

w. You are now finished and can save your manuscript. You should not have to worry again about the compression settings, but the other basic processes you will have to follow for every graphic in your manuscript.

Screen clips

Of course, I did not use screen clips for my novel, but for this book I am using a ton of them. I want to give a brief description of how I made them because I am sure someone will be interested.

The same guidelines apply for the screen clips that applied for the clip art. The screen clip needs to be set at 300 DPI, the screen clip needs to be set at the size it will be in your book, it needs to be grayscale, and saved in the TIFF format. And please, do not forget to turn off Word's compress picture function.

There are also other challenges. To be useful they need circles and captions for the items referred to in the book, and be sharp and readable. To make the screen clips, I used PrintKey 2000 (additional screen clips made for this second edition used the freeware MWSnap). To add the circles and captions, I used Word. Then I used PrintKey 2000 again to take a screen clip of the graphic in Word with the circles and captions. Finally to make it the correct DPI, sharp and readable, I used IrfanView.

a. To make the screen clips more readable, I turned the color scheme of my computer to silver. This helped with the contrast when an icon was selected. On my computer, with a blue scheme the icons turned to a dark square. To make this change, go to **Start Button > Control Panel > Display**. Click the **Appearance** tab, then go down to where it says **Windows and buttons**. Select the **Windows XP** style. Next go down to **Color scheme** and select silver. Click **Apply** then **Cancel**.

b. Your computer is different from mine, especially if you have a different operating system (I am using Windows XP). This means

you will have to explore your computer to find the settings that will give the best contrast.

c. I used PrintKey 2000 to capture many of the screen clips and I used MWSnap for others. PrintKey 2000 was discontinued, so I am using MWSnap for this example. To capture a screen clip using MWSnap, first have on the screen what you want to capture, then click the little MWSnap icon in the notification area (lower right side of your computer). (Your program may have some other hotkey.) On the MWSnap toolbar, click the **Snap any area** icon. The original application will pop back up and your curser will turn into crosshairs. Move the cursor to the top left corner where you want your screen clip to start and click. Then drag it to the bottom right corner where you want it to end and click your mouse button again.

d. As soon as you let up on the mouse button, MWSnap will pop back up showing the clip that you just selected.

e. Next, in MWSnap, go to **Edit > Copy**.

f. Open Word, go to **Page Layout > Page Setup > Small arrow**. Click the **Paper** tab. For doing what we are about to do, I like making the page big, so set the page size to 22 x 22. If you get a message about fixing the margins, click the **Ignore** button.

g. In Word, right click the mouse button and click **Paste**. This should paste the screen clip into Word.

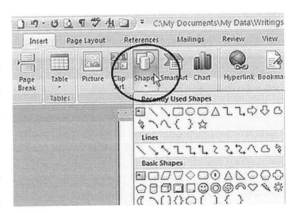

h. Now go to **Insert > Illustrations > Shapes**.

Choose the shapes needed for your graphics. Learning to use these shapes will take some practice, but it is not that hard.

i. Next, right click on each shape. In the menu that will pop up, click **Format AutoShape**. Then find the box that says **Weight**. Change the weight to something larger than one. I used a weight of 1.75 points. The line needs to be thick enough to insure that the printer will print it.

j. If you are trying to circle an item and you need the shape to be transparent, right click the shape, and click **Format Shape**. Then in the **Fill** section of the dialogue box, find where it says **transparency** and slide the bar all the way to the right. That should do it.

k. If you need to add text to one of the shapes, right click the shape and select **Edit Text**.

l. Once you have all the necessary circles, callouts, lines, and text positioned in the graphic, you will use MWSnap again to take a screen shot of it. Click the MWSnap icon in the notification area, then use the **Snap any area** icon to capture the graphic with the newly added items. By doing this, there will be a single graphic that contains an image of the original screen clip and the shapes. Having a single graphic will be much easier to work with and easier for the printer to print.

m. Once MWSnap has captured the screen clip, click the **Copy** icon.

n. Open IrfanView and go to **Edit > Paste**. This will copy the screen clip into IrfanView.

o. In IrfanView, go to **Image > Resize/Resample** and a dialogue will pop up. Below where it says **DPI** change this to three hundred.

Right above this, make sure the two boxes are checked, where it says **Preserve aspect ratio** and **Apply sharpen after Resample**. Next to this to the left, where it says **Size method**, select **Resample**, and choose the slowest method offered, which will probably be the Lanczos filter (the resample filter is the key to making these screen clips look good in print). Now go to **Set new size**, choose **inches**, and change the width to what it needs to be; the height will change automatically. Do not make it too big. Click **Okay**.

p. Now go to **File > Save as.** At the very bottom of the dialogue box, make sure the box for the **Show options dialog** is checked. Then click the down arrow for **Save as type** and choose TIFF. A box will pop up to the right that says **TIFF save options**. The only thing selected should be the one that says **None**. Now give your file a name, find the directory you want to save it in, and save it.

q. Now go to Word and insert it into Word in the same way as with the clip art. Do not copy and paste.

Creating lists

This book uses a lot of lists. By letting Word do the lists for you, you can delete or insert an item and Word will renumber the list for you. You can also—with practice—drag a list item up and down and the list will be renumbered.

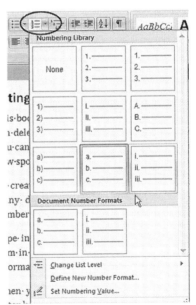

a. To create a list, go to **Home > Paragraph > Numbering**. There are many list styles that can be chosen, choose one and a number or alphabet character will appear to the left of the cursor.

b. Type in your first item, then when you tap the enter key, the next item in the list will be started. In this list, after I finished enter the information for "a.," I tap the enter key and Word created "b."

c. When you finish with the list, tap the enter key and a list item will appear, but then tap the Enter key again or the Backspace key, and that list item will disappear.

d. Using lists are not hard, but they are a little quirky, so take a little time to learn it. Check the list and make sure the numbers are correct. Sometimes it does mess up.

The PDF file

The last step to prepare the internal part of your book is to create the PDF file. This is the type of file Adobe Reader reads. It seems there are different ways to create this file. You can create it for portability—meaning it will be smaller—or you can create it to always display in a certain way, or you can create it to be printed on a commercial printer. Microsoft Office 2007 will save a file as a PDF (you may have to download this add-on from the Microsoft Office website), but I believe that any PDF file you create using the Microsoft Office add-on will be created for portability, which you do not want. I cannot recommend that you use it to create the PDF file for your book. You can give it a go if you like, but I do not have confidence in it. I suspect that it compresses the graphics, which is not good for our purpose. The PDF file I created with novaPDF was 47,578 KB, the PDF file I created using Word's add-on was 3,202 KB. That is a big difference and each PDF file was created using the same Word file. The only way it is possible the Word PDF file is so much smaller is if it compressed the graphics.

You might try freeware PDF creators. There are many of them, but I did not find one that I liked or felt comfortable with. I finally bought novaPDF. I am sure that other programs will do a good job, maybe some of the freeware ones, but I found novaPDF affordable and easy to use.

On my first attempt to create the PDF file, I created my book's PDF files using the Office PDF add-on. I uploaded them to CreateSpace, and they sent me back an email saying that the book cover's PDF file had transparencies in it (which can cause problems for the printer). The files I created using the Office PDF creator looked perfect when I viewed them using Adobe Reader. I then bought novaPDF, and I used it to creating my book cover from the same file. When I viewed it in Adobe Reader, where the title was supposed to be, it was glazed over, and I could not see the words that made up the title. I suspect this is what the printer would have printed. The Word PDF creator did not show this; I believe having a better PDF creator caused this problem to show up. (That block effect resulted because I used WordArt to create the title. The WordArt contained transparencies.)

Having a better PDF creator will also show problems with clip art. Some of the Dover art work had problems displaying in the PDF file. The Dover clip art is quality art, but it is made of many dots and the background sometime bleeds through, which causes the graphic to turn black. I could not see this viewing the file created with the Word's PDF creator, but I could see it with the file created with novaPDF. (I solved this by using the blurring effect in IrfanView.) To repeat myself, I believe the better PDF program did not create these problems, it showed them to me. I am using some transparencies in my books (the clip art), but they can cause trouble and need to be watched.

Creating the PDF file

Once you have finished with your manuscript, you will be ready to create the PDF file. As I said earlier, I am not going to use Word's PDF capability. I am going to use the PDF creator novaPDF, but there are others that I am sure are just as good. If you buy another program to create your PDF file, you will still have to do the same steps that I show you here, but you will have to find these options in your program.

The odd thing about many PDF programs is that they have to be accessed through the print dialogue box of Word and PowerPoint, not the **save** function. The PDF creator will look like a print driver, and you will find it with the print drivers when you print.

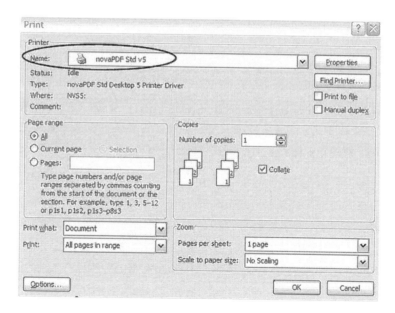

a. In Word, go to **Office Button > Print**.

b. Then under **Printer**, next to **Name**, click the down arrow and select novaPDF.

c. Click the **Properties** button.

d. In the Properties dialogue box, where it says **Graphic** change the **DPI** to **305** and leave the **Scale** at **100**.

e. Under **Orientation,** select the **Portrait** button.

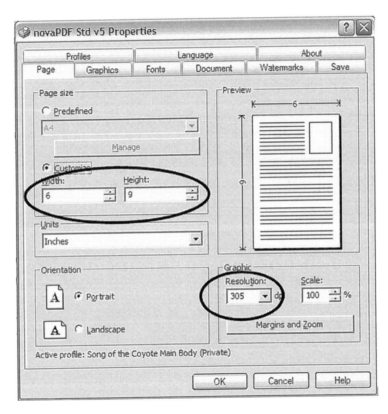

f. Under **Page Size**, click the **Customize** button.

g. Change the width and height to match your book.

h. Width and height settings for *The Song of the Coyote.*

Width > 6	Height > 9

i. Width and height settings for this book.

Width > 8	Height > 10

j. Go to the tab that says **Graphics** and unselect all the boxes. The important goal here is to make sure the PDF creator does not compress and change the DPI of any of the graphics. Your graphics were inserted into the manuscript at 300 DPI, so there is no need for the PDF creator to do anything to them.

k. Next go to the **Fonts** tab. Select **Enable all used fonts**, unselect **Enable font subsets**. On the bottom right side be certain to unselect the **Never embed fonts**. Click **Okay**.

l. Make sure to set the PDF compatibility to Acrobat 5.0 (1.4). In novaPDF go to **Profiles > Profile Name** and then click **Edit**, down where it says **PDF Versions** select **1.4 (Adobe Reader 5)**. Click **Okay** to escape out of the properties dialogue box.

m. In the print dialogue box, click **Okay**. Find the directory where you want to save your PDF file, name the file, and click **Save**; this might take awhile.

n. Now review your PDF file with Adobe Reader. Review every page of it. Take a note of anything that does not look right, then go back into your Word manuscript, correct it, and re-create the PDF file. Do this as often as necessary, until the PDF file looks as you want it to.

o. Once you have finished doing this, you are almost finished with this stage of creating your book. There is one last thing to do. At the bottom of Adobe Reader, where it gives the page numbers, see how many pages your book has and write that down. You will use this

number to calculate the width of your spine. Do not confuse this number with the page number in your footer. The page number in the footer does not include the front matter and may not include some back matter.

Creating the Book Cover

The book cover

We are going to use PowerPoint to create the book cover. The best thing about this is that we get to use PowerPoint. PowerPoint, if you have never used it, is a fun program. It does a good job doing almost everything we need it to do. Creating your book cover is very important and very fun. You will want to take a lot of time and care doing it. PowerPoint will only help. True, PowerPoint was not meant to do this kind of work, and I am sure there are programs that can do a better job—PowerPoint is meant to be used for creating slides for presentations and meetings—but it is affordable and it will work for what we need to do. (Later, I will also introduce Corel Paint Shop Pro, which will do a better job than PowerPoint.)

Another benefit to using PowerPoint is that it makes experimenting with different designs easy. Create a PowerPoint file and on the first slide create some kind of design that you think might look good for your book cover. Anything. Then make a second slide that is a copy of the first slide. In this second slide, make changes that might make it look better. Then on a third slide, try to develop an entirely different design. Keep doing this until you come up with a design you like. You can have as many slides as necessary, each slide a different design. Remember you are just experimenting.

When you come up with a design you like, copy it and put it in a new PowerPoint file. Then see if you can come up with slightly better alternatives to the first slide. Using PowerPoint, you can easily move

from slide to slide to compare them. Do not forget that you have to design the front, spine, and back of the book cover.

Once you know how you want your book cover to look, you can also use PowerPoint to create your book cover. You will have to create a separate PowerPoint file for just this one slide. This slide will be 18 x 12. Inside this slide, we will put a text box that will become your cover. This text box will have to be exactly, EXACTLY, centered in the slide. We will call this the main text box.

The main text box will have to be the correct size. The size is determined by the book size you chose and the number of pages your book has—which determines the size of the spine of your book (the spine is the edge of the book). Using those parameters, we will calculate the exact size the main text box has to be and the inches from the edges of the slide that it has to be to be exactly, EXACTLY, centered. This one text box will include the front of the book, which will be on the right side of the main text box; the spine, which will be in the exact, THE EXACT, center of the main text box; and the back of the book, which will be on the left side of the main text box.

Just to set you at ease, this is not too hard. I will show you how to do the calculations and CreateSpace will calculate the width of the spine for you (but I will show you how). This is much easier than creating headers and footers, I promise.

There are many looks you can give your book cover. Once again, look at other books to get ideas. If you see something you like, you will then have to figure out how to emulate it. My suggestion, if you are not an expert with PowerPoint, is to experiment, use the Internet, use user groups (Also called newsgroups. You can find these using Google Groups), and try to find someone who is knowledgeable with

PowerPoint. Get a good book on PowerPoint, and you may want to take a class.

Much that you will need to know to create your book cover will probably be cover in this book, unless you are using other programs. So before you invest in a class, finish reading this book.

Some of the things I think are important for a cover is balance, correct centering of all the elements, spotlighting what is important, not cluttering the cover with a lot of stuff, and having a nice background. The cover will sell your book, so spend a good deal of time on it.

One warning about PowerPoint: there is no way to lock all the elements in place. Once you have everything positioned exactly where you want them, you cannot lock them so they cannot be moved. Which is another way of saying that they can be moved, even when you do not mean to move them. So every time you mess with your cover file, you must make sure you did not accidentally move the main text box from the center of the slide or the spine's text box from the center of the main text box. You do this by opening the dialogue boxes that control the positioning of the text boxes and make sure none of the position settings have changed.

Is it hard?

Coming up with the design for the book cover might not be so easy. And it may take a while to come up with a good one. You will have to keep at it. Luckily, this is fun work and using PowerPoint is also fun. So although coming up with a good concept for the book cover might be difficult, everything else about the process is not.

The design of your book is limited first by your imagination and second by the capability of PowerPoint. I will not claim that PowerPoint has

the capability of graphic editing programs, but it does work, and it can work well. The cover of the first edition of this book was created using PowerPoint and so was the cover of my novel, *The Song of the Coyote*.

I do not have much advice on the design of your cover. I do advise that you start with something simple and let it grow. Experiment with different designs, using a different slide in PowerPoint for each experiment. Finally, do not over do the design. Remember, the cover should first make people feel good and second compel them to buy the book.

Just as I did not tell you how to write your book, I am not going to tell you how to design your cover either. Instead, I am going to show you how I prepared the cover on my coyote novel, once I figured out how I wanted it to look. The steps I took on my cover should be enough to get you started. To be honest, I am not an artistic person. I am a big believer in simplicity and my cover is simple, which I like. If you are artistic, please feel free to go beyond what I will show you here. You can do much more with your cover that I did with mine. The sky is the limit.

Page setup

a. Open PowerPoint and the first thing you should see is a blank slide, perhaps with the words, "Click to add titles" and "Click to add subtitles." The slide needs to be totally blank, so click several times on the dash lines that

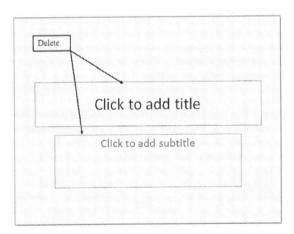

surround those words and delete them by tapping the **delete key**

b. The size of the slide is the same no matter how big or small your book is. The slide has to be 18 x 12. Go to **Design > Page Setup > Page Setup**. A dialogue box will pop up.

c. In the dialogue box, set the width at eighteen inches and the height at twelve inches. Then click **Okay**.

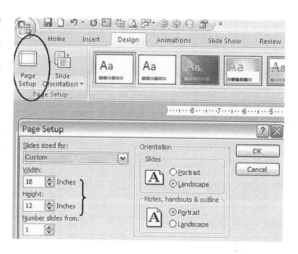

d. What you see next in PowerPoint is probably not 18 x 12. Instead, PowerPoint made the slide fit the screen, which is normally a good thing. But sometimes you need to see it at its actual size. To do that, go to **View > Zoom > Zoom**. Then select the round button in front of 100%. You will see a big white slide.

e. Now click the **Fit to Window** icon, which is next to the **Zoom** icon.

Creating the main text box

Now you will need to create the main text box for this slide. This text box will hold your book cover. In fact, this text box is your book cover. This text box will contain the front of your book, which will be on the right side of the text box. It will contain the spine of your book, which will be in the center of the text box. And it will contain the back cover, which will be on the left side. When printed, the back will be wrapped around the book. Doing all this will require some *easy* math (I am not being sarcastic).

a. To get started, create a small text box by going to **Insert > Text > Text Box**. Click on the slide and a very small text box will pop up.

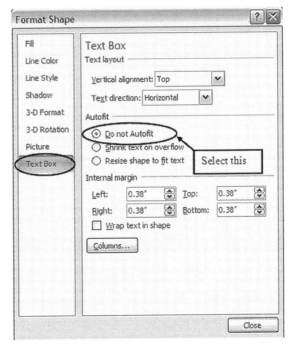

b. Right click on the small text box and go to **Format Shape > Fill > Solid fill**, and select any color you want to fill the text box. This is just temporary so you will not lose the box. You will change the color later.

c. Do not close the dialogue box yet. Go to **Format Shape > Text Box > Autofit**, and select **Do not Autofit**. This is very important because you do not want this text box changing shape.

Determine the size of the main text box

Next we have to figure out the size of the main text box. *The Song of the Coyote* is 6 x 9. The height of the main text box has to be nine inches plus a small trim at the top and one at the bottom (making two trims). The width of the main text box will be the width of the front cover, plus the width of the spine, plus the width of the back cover, plus a trim at the edge of the front cover and a second trim at the edge of the back cover.

The hardest part is figuring out the size of the spine. Again, the spine is the edge of the book, or to put it another way, the spine is how thick the book is.

To calculate the spine, you have to know how many pages your book has and if you are going to use white or cream paper. This book you are reading is printed on white paper; my coyote novel was printed on cream. To find out how many pages your book has, open the PDF file you created for your book and use the number of pages you see at the bottom. The number of pages should include the front material, the body text, and any back material.

My coyote novel had 302 pages (which is 151 sheets of paper). For cream paper, I multiple the total pages with 0.0025. For white paper, I would have multiplied the total pages with 0.002252. If I had chosen white paper the spine would be 302 pages x 0.002252 inch = 0.68 inch. But I did not, I chose cream, so the book spine thickness is 302 pages x 0.0025 inch = 0.76 inch. Notice again that cream paper is thicker than white paper.

One thing to note: The instructions given by CreateSpace say to create an extra outer trim around the cover of 0.125 inch. PowerPoint has problems with the third digit, so I rounded it to 0.13 inch. This creates a trim that is a little larger than what they asked for, but that is okay; it does not hurt if it is a little bigger, just do not make it a little smaller.

Creating the Book Cover

a. Here is a table that shows how the different parts of the cover for *The Song of the Coyote* add up.

Width of book			Height of book	
0.13 (inch)	Left trim		0.13	Upper trim
6.00	Back cover		9.00	Book height
0.76	Spine		0.13	Lower trim
6.00	Front cover		**9.26**	**Total height**
0.13	Right trim			
13.02	**Total width**			

b. Here is a table that shows how the different parts of the cover for this book add up.

Width of book				Height of book	
0.13	Left trim			0.13	Upper trim
8.00	Back cover			10.00	Book height
0.31	Spine			0.13	Lower trim
8.00	Front cover			**10.26**	**Total height**
0.13	Right trim				
16.57	**Total width**				

d. Now right click on the edge of the main text box. Click **Size and Position**, and another dialogue box will pop up.

e. In the tab that says **Size**, the first thing to do is to make sure the box in front of **Lock aspect ratio** is **not** checked.

f. Then in the dialogue box under **Size and Rotate**, the height for my novel will be 9.26 inch and width to 13.02 inch.

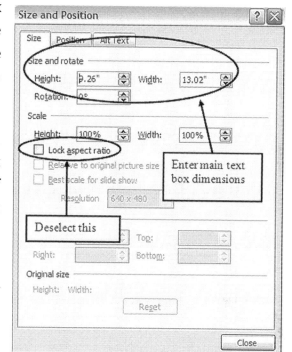

g. Click **Close**. Next we will have to position the text box in the exact center of the slide. More math, but not much.

h. To figure out the horizontal position, take the width of the slide, which is always eighteen inches, subtract the width of the book calculated above, which for my book it is 13.02 inch, then divide by two. That is (18 inch - book width) / 2. For my coyote novel, (18 inch – 13.02 inch) / 2 = 2.49 inch.

i. To figure out the vertical position, take the height of the slide, which is always twelve inches, subtract the height that you calculated above, which for my book is 9.26 inch, and divide by two. That is (12 inch – book height) / 2. For my book, (12 inch – 9.26 inch) / 2 = 1.38 inch (rounded up).

j. Now you need to position the text box in the slide by using these calculations. Right click on the main text box and go down to where

it says **Size and Position**. In the dialogue box, select the tab that says **Position**. For my novel, where is says **Horizontal** enter 2.49 inch. Then where it says **Vertical** enter 1.38 inch. Next to where it says **From**, it should say **Top Left Corner**.

k. Click **Close** and the text box should be centered in the slide. To be sure, you may want to take a measuring tape and measure the gaps around the slide. The top and bottom white margin should be the same, and the left and right white margins should be the same.

l. If you have gotten this far, you should feel good about yourself. You have gotten past most of the confusing stuff. Now you can start the design, which is fun, but I will just warn you, it can also be frustrating.

The background

a. To get started and to give you a good feeling, we will start with the background. Right click anywhere inside the main text box, then go down to **Format Shape**. Click here and a dialogue box will pop up.

b. You will spend a lot of time with this dialogue box. If you have a PowerPoint book, you may want to read up on it. For now, go to **Fill** and then on the right side select **Solid fill** and click the down arrow for **Color** and select a color that you think might look good for the cover. The text box should have change to that color. Notice that outside the text box, the slide did not change color.

c. One note: be careful about using the **Transparency Bar** in any of the options in this dialogue box. In fact, I would avoid using it because it might cause the printer not to print correctly.

The background for *The Song of the Coyote*

For my novel, I filled the main text box with a light brown. But for the bottom, I wanted a darker brown. I did that by creating a second text box, making it as wide as the main text box and several inches high, and then I filled it with the dark brown. To create the mountains, I created another text box using PowerPoint's **Shapes**, selecting the **curve** shape, then I filled it with the same dark brown. My attempt was to create a background that gave an appearance of the ground, mountains, and then the horizon.

a. First, right click somewhere in the main text box, and go down to **Format Shape**. In Format Shape, go to **Fill > Sold Fill** then choose a color. I chose a light brown, which filled the main text box from top to bottom.

b. For the bottom part of the cover, I wanted a darker brown. To do this I created another text box just as I described before. I made this text box as wide as the main text box and about four inches high. I positioned this second text box at the bottom of the main text box. Then I filled this second text box with a darker brown. Now I have a cover with two tones of brown, a light brown up top and a dark brown at the bottom.

c. To create the mountains, I used the PowerPoint's **Shapes**. Go to **Insert > Illustrations > Shapes > Curves**. Then starting at one end of the main text box, right click, then move the line up a little, then right click again, go down a little, then right click, go up a bit, click, and keep doing this until you get to the other end of the main text box. Then bring the line under the mountains and back to the starting point, and click on the starting point. When you manage to click on the starting point, a new text box will be created with the

mountains inside it. I noticed a tendency for this text box suddenly to get longer. Use the shape bars to make it smaller, but it is okay if it extends past the main text box (this extension will not get printed). Then left click it, select **Format Shape**, and fill it with the dark-brown color.

d. Finally, make sure there is not a gap between the mountains and the bottom text box. The two bottom text boxes should look continuous, as if they are one.

Creating the book spine

Creating the book spine will make it possible to put a title on the side of the book. Please keep in mind that CreateSpace recommends that a spine have a title only if the book has more than 130 pages, because of a risk that the title will wrap to the front or back cover. That aside, having a spine, even without the title in it, will help you gauge where to place your cover's graphics and text boxes. More math is involved with creating the book spine, but it is no harder than what you have already done.

To create the book spine we will create another text box, which will sit inside the main text box. You will need to know the width of the spine and the total height of the book; both were calculated earlier. For my coyote book, the spine's width was 0.76 inch and the total height was 9.26 inch. To refresh your memory on this, see the section above, **Determine the size of the main text box.**

a. In PowerPoint, go to **Insert > Text > Text Box**. Click on the slide; you may have to click the part of the slide outside the main text box. You will see a very small text box. For now do not worry about it centering it correctly. Do type in a few temporary letters in it or fill it with a color; otherwise, it might disappear.

b. The next steps are a basic repeat of what we did before. Right click the edge of the spine's text box, and select **Format Shape**. As before, make very sure you go to **Text Box** and select **Do not Autofit**. Still in the **Text Box** section, go down to where it says **Internal Margins**, and set all of them to 0.13 inch. Click **Close**.

c. Now right click the edge of the text box, then go down and click **Size and Position**. First, make sure that the **Lock aspect ratio** option is <u>not</u> selected. Next, change the width to the width of your book spine, then the height to the same height of the main text box. On my book, the width of the spine was 0.76 inch and the height was 9.26 inch.

d. The next thing to do is to position the book spine. It has to be exactly in the center of your book cover. Because you need to be exact, do not just eyeball it, do the calculation. For this step, you have to do just one more calculation because the vertical position is the same as for the main text box, and we already calculated that. For my coyote novel, the vertical position was 1.38 inch.

e. So now we just have to calculate the horizontal position of the spine's text box. To do this use this formula, (18 inch – spine's width) / 2. You will notice this is similar to the formulas that we used before. For my coyote novel, the math will be as follows, (18 inch - 0.76 inch) / 2 = 8.62 inch.

f. Positioning the spine takes the same steps as taken to center the main text box. Right click the edge of the spine's text box, click **Size and Position**, then click the tab at the top that says **Position**. The

horizontal position for my book spine is 8.62 inch. The vertical position is 1.38 inch. The **From** box should read **Top Left Corner**.

g. Click **Close** and your spine should move to the center of your book cover. This is very important, so use your tape measure and measure the distances of the spine from the edge of the slide. It should be the same distance from the left boarder as it is from the right boarder; also it should be the same distance from the top boarder as it is from the bottom boarder. Be certain it is in the center of the main text box. If it is not, make sure the main text box is correctly center. It is **extremely** important these two text boxes be centered correctly in the slide.

Putting the title and name into the spine

The spines of most books, unless they are too thin, have the name of the book and the name of the author.

a. Let us do this so you can see something in your spine. This will help you know where it is when designing the rest of the cover. First, if there are any letters in this text box, delete them. Then go to **Home > Paragraph > Text Direction**, and select **Rotate all text 90**. This will make the text go up and down, instead of side to side as is normal.

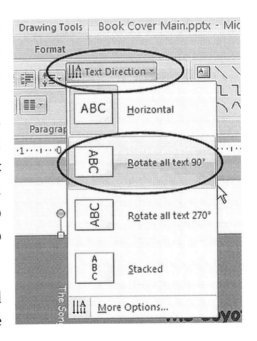

b. Then underneath the **Rotate all text 90** icon, you will see the

Align Text icon, click it. Select **Center** and type the name of your book and your name. Put enough spaces between the title and your name to move the title toward the top and your name to the bottom. For now just make it look good, but before you finish the cover you will want the first letter of the spine's title to be flushed with the top of the front cover's title. You will want the last letter of your name to be flush (or close to flush) with the lowest element of your front cover. On my coyote novel, this last element is the picture of the coyotes howling. This is not an absolute rule, but just a rule of thumb. The big idea is that the title and name in the spine need to be balanced with the front cover (and the back cover).

c. Click the edge of the spine's text box and change the font and point size to a size that fits well in your book's spine.

d. Spine's font and point size for *The Song of the Coyote*.

Font > Comic Sans MS	Font Size > 14 pt

Graphics

Now insert your graphics in the cover. You do this in the same way as was done when inserting graphics into the book's interior. The difference is that you will probably want to use color graphics. Prepare your graphics as described previously, make sure they are set at 300 DPI and that they are the size that you want them to be on the cover. If a graphic's size has to be increased, do it just a little and choose the slowest resample filter. People will judge your book by its cover, so doing a good job is important.

My coyote book has two graphics on the cover, the coyotes singing on the front and a little sparrow on the back. The sparrow on the back, I added as an afterthought because I thought it made the back cover a little more interesting. On the front cover, I used just the one graphic. I had experimented with using several, but I found one that looked good by itself. You can add more graphics if you want. Take your time and make sure they fit together and look good. Try to see your cover as someone who knows nothing about your book. What would they think?

The front cover title and author name

When preparing your cover, remember to stay away from the edges, both outer edges and the edge to the spine; a quarter of an inch should be safe. You can have items that run off the edge if that is what you want them to do, but I have not tried to do that, so I have nothing to say about it.

a. At least two text boxes are needed, one for the title and one for the author's name. Create a text box by going to **Insert > Text > Text Box**. You do <u>not</u> have to go into **Size and Position** as we did before and set the size of the text box or the position. You do <u>not</u> need to select **Do not Autofit**. Unlike the main text box or the spine, exactness is not required and you will have more freedom to move and change the text boxes.

b. In the first text box, I typed in "The Song of," then I tapped the enter key, then I created a bunch of spaces, then I typed "the Coyote." How you design yours will depend on your artistic vision.

c. Once you typed in the title, click the edge of the text box and change the font and the point size.

d. The font and point size of the title of *The Song of the Coyote.*

Font > Comic Sans MS	Font size > 34 pt

e. The font and point size of the titles for this book.

Font > Calibri	Font size top > 54 pt
Font size middle > 40 pt	Font size bottom > 40 pt

f. Now you need to select a color for the title. To do this, double click the edge of the title's text box until the **Drawing Tools Format Ribbon** pops up and go to **Drawing Tools Format > WordArt Styles > Text Fills**. Select a color for the title. For my book, I selected a dark blue. Next, to give the title a thicker look, go just below to **Text Outline** icon. Pick a color that gives the desire effect. Again I chose a dark blue for my book.

g. Next a second text box is needed for the author's name. Create this text box just as you did for the title. Then enter your name. Once again, click the edge of the text box, then change the font and point size. Next, go to **Text Fills** and give the name a color. The name on my coyote novel is a dark blue. I also placed a "~" on both sides of my name because I thought it looked better.

h. The font and point size of the author name of *The Song of the Coyote.*

Font > Comic Sans MS	Font size > 18 pt

i. The font and point size of the author name on this book.

Font > Cambria	Font size > 24 pt

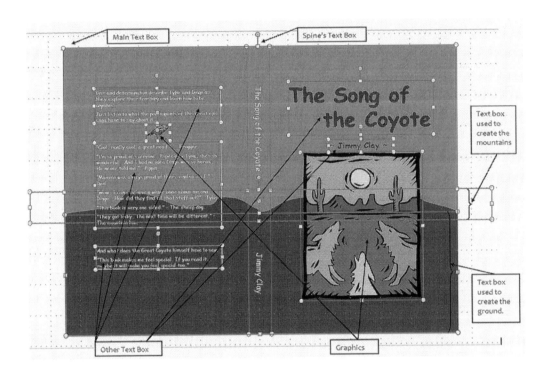

The back cover

If the front cover sells your book by looking good, the back of your book sells your book by appealing to reason. The front of the book should make a potential reader feel good about the book. The back of the book should talk that potential reader into making a commitment to your book by buying it.

Just remember to stay away from the edges, at least a quarter of an inch. Remember to allow plenty of space for the ISBN box, which will be inserted by the printer at the right side of the bottom of the page on the back cover. You do not have to put a ISBN box here, just leave room for it. To give it plenty of room, I would leave an area two and half inches from the spine and one and three-fourths inches from the bottom. That is a little more room than will be needed and you should be safe.

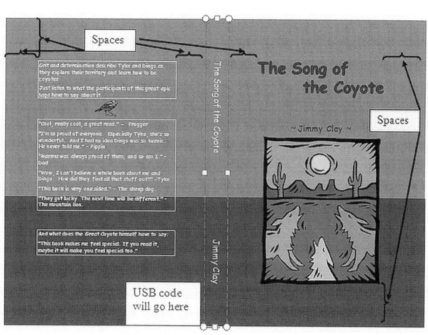

On the back of my coyote novel, I created three text boxes. In the top text box, I said some general words about the novel. In the middle text box, I had some of the characters give brief blurbs about the book. Then in the last text box, I had the Great Coyote give a blurb. I could have included the Great Coyote's blurb in the same text box as the others. The reason I did not is because I felt having three text boxes looked better than just two. That was the only reason.

On the back cover, I have one small graphic, a small sparrow. Although it is small, it is still set at 300 DPI and was inserted, not pasted. The size of the sparrow is the exact size that I reduced it to in IrfanView. I did

not use the graphic handlebars that PowerPoint provides to change the size. I figured out the size the sparrow needed to be by viewing the slide at 100%, then measuring the space between the two text boxes using my tape measure.

Centering elements on the cover

There are two ways to go about centering your graphics and text boxes. You can eyeball them or you can use math. What we are going to do is a combination of both eyeballing and math. We have already done some math, and the math to come is no harder.

With the up and down placement of the graphics and the text boxes, I eyeballed everything. With the centering of the graphic between left and right, math can be a help. The steps are the same for the front cover and the back cover.

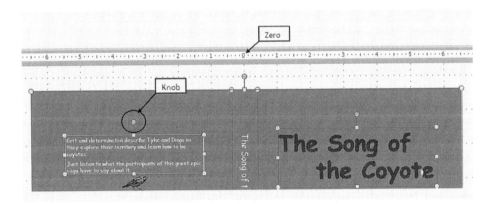

a. The first steps are to turn on the ruler and the gridlines. This is easy because they are located right on top of each other on their ribbon bar. In PowerPoint, go to **View > Show/Hide** and make sure the boxes in front of **Ruler** and **Gridlines** are checked.

b. Now look at the ruler. At the very middle of your slide, it will say zero. If your slide is 18 inches wide, the ruler will show a zero in the middle and countdown to nine going to the right and again going to the left. Here is a second thing to notice. When you move your mouse cursor, in the ruler you will see a little line moving which corresponds to where the cursor is. Now a third thing to notice. If you click on a graphic or a text box, a green knob will appear at the top of the graphic or text box and be exactly in the middle of it.

c. Another thing to notice, if you look at the ruler, each inch is divided into eight notches. Each of these notches is 0.125 inch wide. You can prove this to yourself by dividing one by eight.

d. Here is how I centered the graphic of the three howling coyotes on the front cover of my book. The book cover is six inches wide, so to find the center divided it in half, which is three inches. In addition, there is the book's spine to consider; half of it is to the right of the ruler's zero. The spine is 0.72 inch. Divided that by two gets 0.38 inch. Take that number and add it to the three inches. So 0.38 inch + 3 inch = 3.38 inch. To position the graphic, click on the graphic and the knob appears, then hover the cursor over the knob, position the graphic until the line in the ruler will be on the 3.38 inch mark.

e. You might notice that the PowerPoint ruler does not have decimals, it has eight notches per inch; each of those notches is an eighth of an inch. So how many of those notches are in 0.38 of an inch. Just one of those notches equals 0.125 of an inch. So divide 0.38 inch by 0.125 inch and you will get 3.04 notches. To be centered, the graphic needs to be three inches plus three of those notches to the right of the zero.

f. To center text boxes do the same thing. But first do this, right click the text box and go to **Format Shape > Text Box > Autofit** and select **Resize shape to fit text**. This will ensure that the knob is in the center of the text. Now center the text box just as you did with the graphic.

g. What if you have three columns of graphics on the cover, as this book does? Doing three columns is like what we did above, but might sound more complicated when I explain it. Take the width of the cover as before, but divide by four. Why four? If you have one graphic, divide by two; if you have two columns of graphics, divide by three; and if you have three columns of graphics, divide by four.

h. Then to get the center position for the first column, take the result and add half of the spine's width. To get the center for the second column, take the result, multiply by two, and add half of the spine. To get the third column, take the result, multiply by three, and add half of the spine.

i. This book you are reading is eight inches wide. Dividing that by four gets you two inches. The spine is 0.26 inch, which when divided in half equals 0.13 inch, and that is a little more than one notch mark. To be centered the first graphic needs to be two inches and one notch to the right of the zero. The second row of graphics needs to be four inches and a notch, and the third row of graphics needs to be six inches and a notch. The same is true for the graphics on the back, but going to the left.

j. Does it look right? In the case of this book, I did not think so. The two outside rows of graphics were crowding the middle row. So I moved both the outer rows of graphics two more notches away from the middle row. This gave the middle row room to breathe and looks better. Notice that I moved the outer rows of graphics so they are now a little off centered, and I moved them all an equal amount and I started at their calculated center point.

Creating the book cover PDF file

We are almost finished. Take another look at your cover and make sure you have balanced and artistically placed all the elements. Does it look good? If so, you are ready to create the PDF file

a. Creating the PDF file for your book cover is much like creating it for your interior file. Like before, I used novaPDF to create the PDF file. Set it at 305 DPI, select to **Embed all used fonts**, but selected not to **Embed font subsets**.

b. For the book cover, the orientation should be **landscape**.

c. An important difference is with the page size. The page size will have to be customized, and should be set with the width at twelve inches and height at eighteen inches (no matter what size your book is).

d. If you are still awake, you might have noticed something odd. The width is twelve inches and the height eighteen; logic would dictate that the width should be set at eighteen and the height at twelve. Changing the orientation to landscape seems to be the cause of this flip-flop. If you are using something other than novaPDF, you may not have this problem, experiment with your program.

e. Click **Okay**, then **Okay** again, then navigate to where you want to save the file, then save it with a name of your choice.

f. Take a good look at your cover in Adobe Reader. Does it look right? Do all the elements look balanced? Is the text spelled correctly? Is everything spaced evenly? Do the colors look good? Does it make sense? If you think it is the best you can do, you are ready to upload it to CreateSpace.

Using Paint Shop Pro to Create the Cover

Corel Paint Shop Pro (PSP) is quite different from PowerPoint. Where PowerPoint is fun, PSP is not. Not if you are new to it. If you have been using it for years, I hope you will forgive me. But my introduction to PSP was frustrating, and I think anyone who buys it to create their book cover will experience moments of great frustration. I say this to steal you for the change, not to discourage you.

The cover of the first edition of this book was created with PowerPoint. For the cover of this edition, I used PSP. PowerPoint worked well, and if you only want a basic cover for your book, nothing fancy, then PowerPoint might be all you need. If you do want to get fancy, if you want some texture to your background or if you want a gradient to your background, then I think you need PSP or a similar program.

Of course the program you use does not have to be PSP, but you do need a program that can handle vector and raster graphics. Most important, you need a program that does layers. In fact, a major weakness of PowerPoint for creating book covers is that it does not do layers (of course the creators of PowerPoint did not design it for that purpose). Layers are independent elements on a canvass (the canvass is what you see when creating a new image window in PSP). PSP can flatten the many elements into just one element. A photo taken with a digital camera is a raster graphic with just one element, flatting your book cover will make it a raster graphic with just one element. The commercial printer can have problems interpreting the separate elements in the PowerPoint. By flattening the image to just one element, that problem is eliminated.

Many points that I have to make about the book cover, I already made in the section on PowerPoint. When possible I will not repeat them. By the way, I would advise that you still use PowerPoint to develop your design. PSP is too hard to work with when all you want to do is develop an idea.

PSP is a big program, much too big to be fully covered here. So I am not going to try to. What I am going to try to do is start you in the right direction and tell you the basic process I used, and the solutions to a few of the problems I had. If you have never used PSP before, you will need to get a book on it.

I might have discouraged you from buying PSP, so let me add that it does get easier. You will have to spend a goodly amount of time learning it and playing with it. If you live near a college, you might want to check if they offer any courses on PSP. If they do not offer a course for it, they might for Photoshop Elements, which is the same type of program as PSP. I have never used Photoshop Elements so I have no opinion about it, but you might consider buying it instead.

Top things to remember about PSP

Below are a few things to know that might make your first encounter with PSP less stressful. These are intended for those who have never used PSP before.

a. It does get easier, but I strongly advise that when you start learning PSP, that you remove all guns, sharp and pointy objects, and rope from your home.
b. PSP does not have the dialogue boxes that PowerPoint has to control where you place text boxes and images. Yes, this is annoying. There are tricks to get pass this problem.

c. There is no importing of graphics into PSP. Each graphic has to be opened in its own window, fixed the way it needs to be, then copied and pasted to the book cover window.

d. When doing a copy, do a simple copy such as ctrl-c. Do not use the **Copy Special** options. They are not necessary and can make your image smaller when pasted.

e. PSP does have a type of text box; it is not as easy to work with as a text box in PowerPoint. I advise creating all your text—the title, author name, spine text, description on the back cover—in separate windows. I think it is much easier to work with the text in a separate window, then copy and paste the text to the book cover window.

f. With Word and PowerPoint I stressed not to use the resize handles. With PSP that does not hold true, use the handles. PSP will automatically resample the image if you resize it with the handles. Remember that you will still risk losing image quality if you make an image bigger.

g. PSP's ruler will give the size of the picture in inches that it will be when printed, not the size it is on your screen. If you specify a graphic to be two inches wide with a 300 DPI, it may appear much bigger on your screen. On my screen, that graphic is six inches long (even though it will print two inches long). This is because a two-inch wide graphic with 300 DPI is 600 pixels wide. On my computer 600 pixels takes up six inches.

h. Save often. PSP tends to hang up.

i. Here is a little terminology to avoid confusion (I hope) for those new to computers. When you do a **File > New** in PSP, you will create a **New Image**. It says so at the top of the dialogue box that pops up. This new image will have a checkerboard canvass when you first open it. The checkerboard is called the canvass. Notice the new image is also a new window in PSP. In PSP an image, canvass,

and a window can be the same thing. When you save this image/canvass/window on your computer, it will be a file. The same thing can be called a new image, canvass, file, or window. We will simply call it a window, such as "create a new image window." The file that contains your book cover will be called the "book cover window" when it is open in PSP.

j. One more terminology. I use the term "elements" to refer to all the separate things you will be adding to your book cover. The spine, the graphics, the text boxes with the title, your name, and descriptions, I call all of those things elements. Notice also that each element will be in its own layer, until you merge them.

Basic strategy

Here is the strategy. If you know PSP already, this might be all the information you need. The first step is to create a new image window that has the width and height of your book cover. Give this new image window a DPI of three hundred, make it raster background, and select the color depth of "RGB – 8 bits/channel."

The second step is to change the background to a color and to give it whatever affects you want. You can even make a picture your background. Be creative. One thing I have observed is that no book that I have found uses the type of texture that looks like wallpaper, so be careful about that. Most backgrounds have a few sold colors, a gradient, or will have some kind of cloud effect.

The Third step is to create the spine so you can see where the center is. Do this by opening a new image window, make it the size you calculated your spine to be, with a 300 DPI. To make it easier to enter the name of book and your name in the spine, I recommend you place the height of your spine in the width box and the width of your spine in the height box. How weird, right? This will make the spine appear long way. Once you have entered the book name and your name in the spine, you can then rotate it so it will be correctly aligned. Merge the spine's text layers to its background layer, copy the entire spine window, and paste the spine to the book cover window as a new layer. It will paste exactly in the middle of the window, which is where you want it. When doing the next step, step four, knowing exactly where the spine is will make placement of the other elements easier. Before doing the above, it can be helpful to create a temporary spine with a solid color that stands out, then when all the other elements are in place, delete the temporary spine and then place the real spine.

The fourth step is to add all the elements—the text, the graphics, and on the cover of this book, the six banners. Turn on the grid and align all the elements.

The fifth step is to merge everything. The book cover window needs to be one layer.

The sixth step is to create a new image window that is eighteen inches wide and twelve inches high and 300 DPI. Make the color of this image white. Then go back to the book cover window, copy it, then paste it to the new image window as a new layer. It should copy exactly to the center. Once you are convinced it is centered, merge the layers (there will probably be two) to just one.

The seventh and last step is to create your PDF file. Do this just as explained for PowerPoint.

That is all there is to it.

Creating a new image

If you do buy PSP or some similar program, you almost will have to buy a book on it. I bought one for PSP, but I only sort of like it, so I cannot fully recommend it. One important advantage to Photoshop Elements is there are more books written on it. That is not what I bought; I bought PSP and that is the program used here. To help you get started, I am going to show you the basic steps I took to create the book cover for this book. The first step is to create a new image window that will contain the book cover.

a. Go to **File > New** and a **New Image** dialogue box will pop up.
b. Under **Image Dimensions,** enter the width and height of your book, just as done with PowerPoint (use the same values used for the main text box in PowerPoint). For resolution, select 300 pixels per inch.

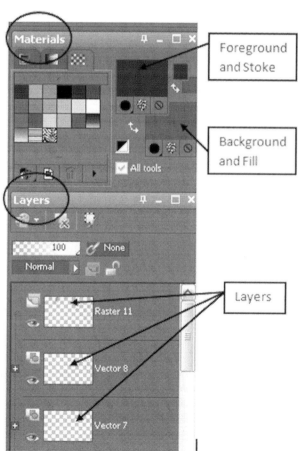

c. Under **Image Characteristics,** select **Raster Background**. For **Color depth** select **RGB – 8 bits/channel**. For **Color,** check the **Transparent Box**. Use these settings for all new images.

d. Next click **Ok.**

Creating the background

a. Go to **View > Palettes**, click on **Materials** and while you are there click on **Layers**.

b. To understand fully the **Materials** box, you will need a book on PSP. This box can take different looks depending on how you have PSP setup, but it should have two color boxes that are bigger than the others. Clicking on either of those boxes will bring up a **Material Properties** dialogue box. Click the top box (**Foreground and Stroke Properties**) and set it to the color you want the background to be. If you used PowerPoint to develop your book cover and you want to use the same color in PSP, you can enter the **Red, Green, Blue** values here. The first edition of this book had values of Blue 37, Green 64, and Blue 97. I am keeping those values here. Click **Ok**.

c. Then click the second box (**Background and Fill Properties**) and change the color of this box to the color you want the text to be.

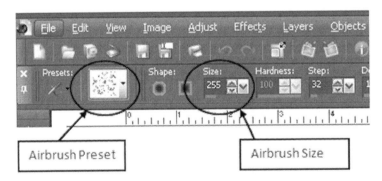

d. The image window is probably a white and gray checkered pattern. To change this to the color of the top box, go to the **Tools Toolbar**, probably to the far right. Find the **Flood Fill Tool** and click on it. Then left click the white and gray checkered pattern. It should change colors. For this book, it changed to a blue.

e. Next to give the background some texture (there might be a million ways to do this but I am going to show how I did it), click the top color box again and change it to a lighter shade of the original color. I changed mine to Red 38, Blue 84, and Red 134. Click **Ok**.

f. Now go to the **Tools Toolbar** and find the **Airbrush** tool and click it. Next, you may need that book on PSP to understand this part, but go to the **Palette Toolbar** and select the **Preset** down arrow. For this book, I chose **Marble 2**, and made it as big as possible. Next click the book cover and a texture will be "sprayed" on the background. Do the whole cover this way. When you finish, be sure to **Save**.

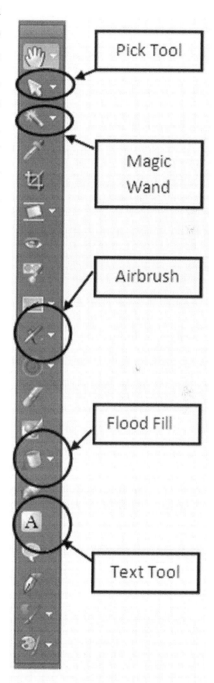

Creating the spine

a. Go to **File > New** and a **New Image** dialogue box will pop up.

b. Enter the values you calculated for your spine, except place the width of your spine as the **Height** and the height of your spine as the **Width**. Keep all the other values the same as for the background. Click **Ok** and a new image window will pop up, and it should be the long way.

c. For now, use the **Flood Fill Tool** to set the background of your toolbar to a color other than the background color of the book cover. The purpose is to make the spine visible. Doing this will help you place the other elements in the book cover. So fill the spine with black or red or some other color, then **Rotate** it so it is correctly aligned (the rotate icons are on the top toolbar). Go to **Edit > Copy**, then go to the book cover window and do an **Edit > Paste As New Layer**. The spine will paste on your book cover exactly in the center, which is where you want it.

d. Notice too that there are now two layers in the **Layer Palette**. When you have finished adding all the elements to your cover, you will have to delete this temporary spine layer and add the permanent spine. If you have added everything you want to the book cover window and have aligned them (let us assume you have), click the spine's layer in the **Layer Palette** and delete it.

e. Now to create the permanent spine with the book's name and your name. Create a new image just as you did before, with the spine's dimensions as the values, but with the width and height swapped.

f. Make sure the lower color box in the **Materials Palette** is the color that you want your text to be. Now go to the **Tools Toolbar** and select the **Text Tool**. I found this to be an unfriendly tool, so you will just have to work with it until it does what you want. Click the spine where you want the book name to be. A **Text Entry** box will pop up. Before you enter any text, set the font and point size. Next enter the book name and then click **Apply**. Next click the spine where you want your name to appear and repeat the above steps.

g. Align the book name and your name. Select the **Pick Tool** in the **Tool Toolbar**, click on the book name, then hold down the **Shift Key** and click on your name. A dash box should form around the book name and your name. Now go to **Objects > Align > Vert. Center in Canvas**. Both names should be aligned to the center of the spine. Leave the background transparent.

h. Now click the **Rotate Right** icon to align the spine correctly.

i. Now copy your spine and paste it to the book cover window as a new layer. It should paste at the centered.

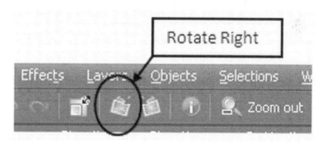

j. Now click on the book name in the spine and move it up or down until the first letter is even with the title on the front cover. Now do the same for the author's name in the spine; move it until is balanced with the lower elements on the front cover; use your artistic judgment. You may have to repeat step g.

Creating text

Creating the text for your cover is basically the same as creating the text for the spine. You will need to create a new image window for each text element. Do all the work that you need to do to the text in this separate window, then copy the text window to the book cover window. Once you have done this work, save the text window to your computer (it should be in its own file), just in case you need it again (i.e. you mess up).

a. Create a **New Image** window. The dimensions should be the approximate size that you believe the text will occupy in the book cover.

b. Select the **Text Tool** and click on the new image window. The **Text Entry** dialogue box will open. Select your font and pint size, type your text, then click Apply.

c. Use the **Pick Tool** to center the text. Use the handles on the text box to make the text box the same size as the canvas. If the canvas is too big, go to **Image > Canvas Size** to resize the canvas.

d. If you want to change the font or point size, highlight all the text in the **Text Entry** dialogue box and then change the font or point.

e. Copy and paste the text image window to the book cover window. Use the **Pick Tool** to position it. Use the handles to fine tune the size of the text box in the book cover window.

Graphics

Working with graphics is similar to text. You will have to open each graphic in its own window. As much as possible, use vector graphics. This is not always possible, and if any of the PSP affects are used on a vector graphics, such as the airbrush, PSP may require you to convert it to a raster graphic. Nevertheless, vector graphics have many advantages, so use them when you can. If PSP requires you to convert to raster, be sure to size the graphic before it is converted.

a. Open the graphic and resize it. Remember if it is a vector graphic, it can be resized without losing quality, but if it is a raster graphic, it will lose quality if made larger.

b. For raster graphics, to make a background transparent do this: Right click the image and select **Promote Background Layer**. In the **Tools Toolbar**, find the **Magic Wand Tool**. Click the part of the background that you want to be transparent. You should see a moving line outlining the background (not all graphics will confine this moving line to the area where you want it). Tap the **Delete** key and that part of the image should disappear, leaving the deleted area with a checkerboard. Click any other part of the graphic that should be transparent and delete that area too.

c. Make any other changes the graphic needs.

d. Save this window to its own file, just in case you need to use it again.

e. Now copy and paste the graphic window to the book cover window. The graphic's background should be transparent if you performed step b.

f. Use the **Pick Tool** to position the image.

g. Now do this process for all the graphics that will be on the cover.

Aligning text and graphics

a. If you are using vector elements on your book cover, you can try to use PSP alignment tools. Use the **Pick Tool** to select the elements that need to be aligned (hold down the shift key), then go to **Object** menu and choose a command in either the **Align** or **Distribute** submenu.

b. If you cannot get the above to work or if you are using raster graphics, you will have to eyeball it. There are some things you can do to help you line up all the elements, but mostly you will have to use your artistic senses.

c. Use the math discussed under PowerPoint to get the center points. This will help you get going.

d. Make sure you can see the spine.

e. Turn on the ruler. Go to **View > Ruler**.

f. When you are aligning, turn on the grid. Go to **View > Grid**.

g. Work to create balance.

h. Good luck.

Merging

Once you have your book cover just as you want it, the next step is to merge all the layers. This is what makes PSP better than PowerPoint. If you created your book cover with PowerPoint, the PDF file would have contain many elements that the printer would have to interpret. I used PowerPoint to create the cover for the first edition of this book, so it can work. But merging is better. The PDF file created from PSP will have just one element.

a. Before you merge, save the book cover window to a different filename. If you do not like your cover when you see the proof copy, you can go back to the original file, with all the layers, to make changes.

b. In the new book cover window, go to **Layers > Merge > Merge All**. In the **Layers Palette,** you should see one layer.

c. Save.

Next to the last step

You have one more thing to do before creating the PDF file. This is easy.

a. Open a new image window. Give it the same values as the other new images you created, but the size should be twelve inches high and eighteen inches wide.
b. Make the canvas white.
c. Now for the big step. If it is not already open, open the file that has your book cover in it, the one with all the elements merged to one layer.
d. Copy this file by going to **Edit > Copy**.
e. Go back to the image window you just created. Go to **Edit > Paste As New Layer**. It should paste exactly in the middle of the canvas (do not move it!). You should see two layers in the **Layers Palette**.
f. Now do this. Go to **Layers > Merge > Merge All**. You should now just see one layer.
g. Save.
h. Now, from this file, create the PDF file.
i. Hum, maybe I was wrong, maybe PSP is not that hard.

Creating the PDF file

There is only one change from how we created the PDF file with PowerPoint. I am only going to cover this one point.

There is a limit to how large your cover PDF file can be; it can only be 40 megabytes. The cover file for this book was close to 56 megabytes. To reduce the size of the file, I compressed it, which reduced the size to only 7 megabytes. Quite a change.

a. In PSP, go to **Print > novaPDF > Properties > Graphics**. Select **Compress high color images** and configure it to **JPEG (Maximum)**.
b. None of the other Graphics options should be selected.
c. Now proceed just as you did with PowerPoint.

Conclusion

Although it can be frustrating, I hope you have discovered that what we have just done is not that hard. It is very doable. Certainly it is not as hard as writing the book. It takes some time and patience, a lot of patience. What is important is you can do it, and I hope this book makes it easier for you.

Once you have your book prepared and published on Amazon, you can do one more thing. Submit your book to Amazon's Kindle program. This will published your book in the Kindle format so it can be read with the Kindle Reader. This is easy to do, providing you are not submitting any graphics. Unlike the printed book, my Kindle file for my coyote novel does not contain any graphics. The Kindle program is free for writers who want to publish with it, and you will earn revenue on each book downloaded to a Kindle reader, so it is worth doing.

Good luck and happy publishing.

The Song of the Coyote

A Classic Tale of Wisdom, Love, and Adventure

"The best fun I've had in a long time." - the old coyote

"I wish I had written this book." - the wise coyote

"Tyke and Dingo are heroes that all young coyotes can emulate. This classic made me proud to be a coyote." - The Coyote Wildlife Guild *

* The Song of the Coyote is a proud supporter of The Coyote Wildlife Guild and their philosophy of wildlife management, except for the part about leaving your pet cat outside. We also recommend that you keep a watch on small dogs.

The Coyote Wildlife Guild

Coyotes, we protect the wildlife so you don't have to. Trust us.

Help us, help you, save the wild.

What we believe*:

- Let your cat outside. Every house cat is a wildcat wanting to let loose.
- Keep sheep sheared. All that fur upsets the stomach.
- Keep our wildlife beautiful. Pick up all metal objects such as, cans, wire, and traps.
- Keep your dogs indoors (unless they are small). They release way too much methane, another cause of global warming.
- Grow a garden. Carrots are the best food to grow, lattice too.
- Field mice are not bad. They are cute and have soft bodies. They are a natural part of the ecology.

* Please support The Wildlife Coyote Guild by following these core principles.

10107096R0

Made in the USA
Lexington, KY
24 June 2011